If You Think You Are My Daughter

Karen Sweet and Jeanne Biedrzycki
as told to Lewis M. Elia

Printed in Victoria, Canada

National Library of Canada Cataloguing in Publication

Sweet, Karen
If you think you are my daughter / by Karen Sweet and Jeanne Biedrzycki ; as told to Lewis M. Elia.

ISBN 1-4120-0795-X

I. Elia, Lewis M., 1935- II. Biedrzycki, Jeanne III. Title.

HV874.82.S93A3 2003 362.82'98'092 C2003-903987-0

TRAFFORD

This book was published *on-demand* in cooperation with Trafford Publishing.
On-demand publishing is a unique process and service of making a book available for retail sale to the public taking advantage of on-demand manufacturing and Internet marketing. **On-demand publishing** includes promotions, retail sales, manufacturing, order fulfilment, accounting and collecting royalties on behalf of the author.

Suite 6E, 2333 Government St., Victoria, B.C. V8T 4P4, CANADA
Phone 250-383-6864 Toll-free 1-888-232-4444 (Canada & US)
Fax 250-383-6804 E-mail sales@trafford.com
Web site www.trafford.com TRAFFORD PUBLISHING IS A DIVISION OF TRAFFORD HOLDINGS LTD.
Trafford Catalogue #03-1163 www.trafford.com/robots/03-1163.html

10 9 8 7 6 5

This book is dedicated to my parents

Harold and Mary Lou Leiser.

"The greatest gifts I ever got
came from heaven
and I call them mom and dad."

Karen

Acknowledgments

Karen and Jeanne would like to thank the following people:

Kevin Sweet and Paul Cohen. They were the pillars of strength who held us up during this time and whose constant love and support continue to endure.

Pat Rutherford of World Wide Tracers, Inc. for the sensitivity he showed in handling this case and for his contribution to this book.

Our chronicler, Lewis M. Elia (Karen's father-in-law) whose initiative, direction, and expertise as a published author helped to make this book exceed our expectations.

Our families and friends, too numerous for us to mention here, whose support and encouragement for this project is appreciated.

Lewis would like to thank his wife, Linda (Kevin's mother) for her support and help which is always there for us.

Credits:
Back Cover:
Ashokan Spring: from a pastel by Robert Selkowitz
Sunlight Studio
3024 Rt. 28, Ashokan, New York
845-657-6982 www.artfolks.com
(used by permission)

INTRODUCTION

I have completed over 16,000 adoption cases in my twenty-two years of uniting adoptees and birth parents, and this case is my all-time favorite. It has everything. It is the story of Jeanne, a sixteen-year-old girl who gave birth to a daughter, had it taken away from her, and was told that she would never see her daughter again. It tells of her suffering and tears as she grew older, and how everything that happened in her life would bring back the memories of the precious baby she never saw and would never get to meet. It tells of the six years she would spend searching for the child and how many times she would be told she had no right to find her, in spite of the fact that she never willingly gave her up. Her sin was being too young to have any control over what happened to her daughter.

Finally she gave up searching on her own and called me. The State of New York was extremely difficult when it came to opening records for birth moms. Jeanne told me that her own mother had cervical and breast cancer which did not take her life, but she eventually died of a heart attack. Now she was even more determined to find her daughter in order to make her aware of this. The medical history was what we needed. That, of course, was enough to petition the court, even though in New York it was extremely difficult to do. The child had a right to this knowledge. The case was heard by a caring judge who ordered the records unsealed and appointed me as the intermediary. When I told Jeanne about the judge's decision, I had never heard anyone express such joy.

The next step was to find Karen, the birth daughter. To be honest, I expected a resounding "Yes, I want to see my mother!" Instead, I was told "No, I already have a mother." I could tell by her voice she was the image of Jeanne, and I could sense her sweetness and tenderness over the telephone. She, however, would not give in, as she did not want to hurt her adoptive parents. I was disappointed. I felt as if I had made no impact on her and could not change her mind. I even talked to her new husband, but it seemed to me that nothing worked.

Jeanne was devastated, as was I. She did not know that as she was crying on one end of the phone, tears were also streaming down mine on this end. I told her to be patient. This was obviously a shock to Karen, and I felt that if some time passed it could still prove to be a good reunion. However, my words sounded hollow even to me.

A few days later my phone rang, and it was Karen. The result is the touching story that follows. After you read it, you will understand why I say this is my favorite case and why, even at the age of seventy-five, I will never stop reuniting birth mothers and daughters.

This story is a must read for anyone, especially those who have given up a child, those who have been adopted, or those who are adoptive parents.

Pat Rutherford
Private Detective, World Wide Tracers, Inc.
http://www.worldwidetracers.com
March, 2003

PREFACE

My daughter-in-law, Karen was adopted at birth. After thirty years her birth mother, Jeanne found her. I had already met Jeanne a few times, but it was at my grandson Brendan's second birthday party that I really got a chance to talk to her. I have an adopted son of my own, Peter and I was curious to know how Jeanne had gotten through the maze of New York State's adoption laws to find Karen, the daughter she was forced to give up over thirty years ago. I found their story so fascinating, I convinced them to share it. They had been reunited for five years and luckily they had saved all the letters, cards, photos, and e-mails pertaining to their story which, I reasoned, would make it much easier to tell.

We all decided that I would act as chronicler for their journey and put together a book for them, since I am a writer. In the meantime they would gather all the items they had saved and put them in order. I would take the responsibility of writing the narratives, which would give deeper meaning to the story based upon interviews, personal notes, photos, and anything else they could think of.

They had a lot to think about. Sometimes they were able to write out or express their feelings, and other times I had to dig deeper to get at them.

This book then is a chronicle of two women making a search. Jeanne's search is an unrelenting physical and spiritual journey to find a lost child. Karen's search is a spiritual one, a coming of age which tears into her good life and forces her to confront adversity. Both insist they have become better people for the experience. Both say they have learned a great deal about people, family, and love. I thank them both for giving me the privilege of telling their story, because I have learned a great deal about these subjects too.

Lewis M. Elia
March, 2003

My parents were good people. They were very honest and hard-working. My father was a dairy farmer and my mother a homemaker. They led a simple life on the farm and were always happy together. They never intentionally hurt anyone and always provided for their family. They always did the best they could to make life better for their children, and for the most part they did. Mom was raised in a large Irish Protestant family in South Carolina. Dad was raised in a large Polish Catholic family. However, he had a problem relating to the precepts of the Catholic faith, and upon marrying my mother decided to break away from the church. They joined a nearby Dutch Reformed church when they bought their first farm. Dad worked the farm by himself, milking and attending to the cows every day. Mom would help with some of the farm work but spent most of her time taking care of us and the house. My father rarely took time off. They attended church only on the holidays.

I was the middle of three sisters, five years apart in age, and we grew up on our dairy farm in upstate New York. Few people, if any, get rich on a farm, but we never wanted for anything. My parents worked hard and made many sacrifices to provide a good home for their children. My sisters and I always ate well and were adequately dressed. We wore a lot of hand-me-downs from our well-to-do cousins in the South. We didn't mind. We had plenty of toys, but not so many as the kids of today. Television had just become available in the early 1950s and the choice of programs was very limited, so we mostly played outside and helped with household chores. We never missed going to Sunday school.

Dad was a very quiet, introspective man of few words. He rarely became angry and almost never raised his voice. He had an unhappy childhood, which he rarely mentioned. But when he did, he said his stepfather was mean to him. When my father was very young, his own father died during the 1917 influenza epidemic. His stepfather forced him to quit school in the ninth grade and made him work on the farm. My father always resented him for that. But, he never complained. Dad was very easy-going and generally went along with anything my mother wanted to do. She never demanded much, and I think he just wanted to keep the peace and always make sure she was happy.

I can still remember when Dad would come in the house exhausted after a long day. He would usually fall asleep on the couch until dinner. There was often little conversation except between my sisters and me. I know my parents were happy together, but I also know they always had to struggle and life was never easy for them. Through a child's eyes, it seemed as if there wasn't much time for laughter, fun, or excitement. And to me, life always appeared difficult and mundane.

I'm sure when we were little my father was more affectionate, but it is hard to remember. I know he loved us all very much, but found it difficult to express his feelings. He wasn't the type who would kiss and hug us or make a big fuss. What I do remember is sitting on his lap and giving him a kiss and hug goodnight. I also remember some of the special toys he made for us, including a doll cradle and playpen, a teeter toter and a swing. I realize that this was his way of expressing love.

My mother was the opposite. She was very loving and affectionate, especially when we were young. She had a difficult childhood as well. Her father also died during the 1917 influenza epidemic. She was one of five children, and her mother worked two jobs to support the family. She spent a lot of time with her older siblings and grandparents, who helped to raise her. For this reason, I think she became somewhat overprotective of her own children. She was always afraid of us getting hurt. She did everything to protect us and make our lives better than her own childhood had been. She was very unselfish, and deprived herself of many things in order to give her children things that she'd never had.

Growing up on a farm was generally a good thing. There were cows, horses, cats, and dogs to play with. School days were not much different for us than other farm children attending public school in the 1950s. I did well in school, always had my homework done on time, always did exactly what the teacher told me, and never caused any trouble. I was an average kid. I was kind of shy. I wouldn't describe myself as really popular, but I was not unpopular. Generally, I believe just about everyone liked me. I certainly don't think anyone disliked me. My best friend since kindergarten (I'll call her Jane) lived just down the road from my house. Having a sister five years older and another five years younger was not the same as having a friend your own age. Jane and I saw the world the same way. We figured things out together and were always there for each other. We had no secrets, and talked about how cute John in the third row was and how we were sure that Mrs. A., the music teacher, wore a wig. We would sing out of tune just to annoy her. I stayed overnight at Jane's house all the time. Her sister was much older and had moved out of the house, so we were pretty much inseparable.

Jane could talk to her mother about a lot more things than I could talk with my mother about. Her mother was a nurse and so I assume that she must have had some sort of mother--daughter talk at some point. But I couldn't think about discussing these things with my mother. Of course, there was no sex education in school in those days, and my older sister was not much help. My mother never explained anything to her either. Therefore, I knew little or nothing about boys and sex.

I remember the first time I got my period. It was a very frightening experience. I thought I was going to die. I can't remember the explanation my mother gave me. It was all very vague and mysterious to me. Somewhere along the line, I guess I figured out that boys get girls pregnant. But surely this wouldn't happen to me, at least not until I got married. Then I would have a family and live happily ever after. That's just the way it was. There wasn't any other way.

My parents always attended important school and church functions that we participated in, although, their involvement with our other activities was limited. As my sisters and I grew older and ventured out on our own, my parents were often naive and not always aware of the temptations that awaited teenagers, particularly young girls. It was the early 1960s and the world was changing. It was very different from when they were growing up. Unfortunately, it was difficult for them to relate to all of this. My parents and I couldn't seem to talk to each other.

All this was happening just as America was about to shed its post-war Puritanism and enter a sexual revolution. Being a 1950s farm girl did not prepare me for what was about to happen. Mini- skirts and fishnet stockings were the rage, and suddenly I was getting lots of attention from boys. By the time I was fifteen, I'd met a boy who was much older. He was the same age as my older sister and was very handsome and self-assured. I was totally in love and would do anything for his attention. As I reflect back on that time, I realize how naive and vulnerable I was. The combination of hormones raging in my fifteen-year-old body, being told I was beautiful, and living the dream of a man who loved me, made me feel wonderful. It was too much for me to resist. The "new morality," which said it was all right to express your feelings sexually, contributed to that fateful evening when my "white knight" swept me off my feet. I never felt so loved and wanted in my life. Then reality struck. I found out I was pregnant.

When I told my parents, I could see the strain on their faces. They reacted with the typical restraint they always placed upon their emotions. However, they couldn't hide the concern in their eyes. Naturally, the only honorable thing to do was to get married.

The thought of getting married was a frightening prospect to a sixteen-year-old. But I thought it was the only thing to do. Sure, my husband and I would struggle for awhile, but eventually we would make it. I would have to quit school, but my family would help as much as they could. It was the only solution. Until we found out that my boyfriend was seeing another girl.

And so the dream ended. Seeking advice from the high school principal, my parents decided that putting the child up for adoption was the only sensible thing to do. It was impossible to keep the baby. They would not hear of it. With my dream shattered, my parents made arrangements for me to be admitted to a home for unwed mothers. We drove to Tarrytown, New York for a preliminary visit.

I clearly remember the overwhelming sense of dread that I experienced during the entire trip. I remember little else except walking in the front door of this very large old home, which felt dark and cold inside. My memory during my entire pregnancy fades in and out. I recall feeling that I wished time would stand still and give me more time to think. I felt confused; everything was happening too quickly. Decisions were being made for me. What would happen to my baby? I can also clearly recall the first time I began to feel my baby move. It was a special moment that is difficult to put into words. The bond and the connection had definitely begun.

It was June 22, 1967 when the labor pains began. I had terrible back pain. It was too early for the baby to be born, but the pain didn't stop. My mother decided we had to go to the local hospital. It was too far to drive to Tarrytown, and it wasn't worth taking the chance. After a very long labor, I was given a general anesthesia and my baby was born at 3:04 a.m. on June 23, 1967. The papers were prepared and the baby was put up for adoption. I was still under the influence of anesthesia when I signed the final papers. I clearly remember tears rolling down my face and pleading with the social worker, "Please make sure you find my baby a good home."

I never saw her. I couldn't help wondering what she looked like, how she sounded when she cried, who was giving her comfort. Not seeing her was the worst part. I wondered if she looked like me. I could only hope that when she grew up and was old enough to know she was adopted, she would understand why I couldn't keep her. When I arrived home there was an overwhelming sense of loss. It felt as if somebody had died. I felt completely numb. I can remember staring out the window of my room for hours. Nothing looked the same anymore. Suddenly everything had changed, and I was a different person. No one ever spoke of the situation again. It was our secret, which I would have to live with forever.

I returned to school that fall, not prepared for what would happen. My best friend Jane would not talk to me. I felt like an outcast. Most people were polite, but few wanted to associate with me. I felt abandoned and worthless. Yet I had to go on. My parents were still there for me, but they were also having a difficult time coping with the situation. I really needed counseling, but there was no one to help. I had to make it on my own.

I graduated from high school, went on to nursing school, and became an RN. I thought a change would help me through the hurt. I moved to Florida for ten years, and then to California. The shame and guilt followed me. I had a difficult time trusting men. I made it my goal to become independent. I would never need anyone again. There was no white knight or fairy tale; no one would ever fool me again.

It was 1991 and life in California was good, but I began feeling an overwhelming desire to return home. I decided to move back to upstate New York. It was a good move for me. Mom was happy that I had returned, and we began to get closer.

After being home for three years, my world was shaken when my mother, who had earlier beaten cancer, suddenly died of heart attack on Christmas Day, 1994. Her death brought back all the feelings of loss I experienced when I lost my child. I felt like the world was crashing in on me. I loved my mother. I thought about the mother--daughter relationship. I thought about the fact that I had a daughter--yet I didn't have a daughter. I thought about dying without my daughter knowing anything about me. I knew I had to find her.

I have always known I was adopted. My brother is also adopted and my parents never hid that fact from us. They have a biological child, my younger sister Annie, and it never occurred to us that we were not blood siblings. I never really knew exactly what it meant to be an adopted child until I grew much older. I was always surrounded by family: a brother and sister, cousins, aunts, uncles, and grandparents. They were all aware of my brother and me being adopted, but no one ever made us feel unloved or unwanted. We just belonged, and adoption was simply a natural thing.

We heard the usual things adopted children hear when they are growing up: "You don't look like your parents," or, "You and your sister don't look as if you are related." Feeling uncomfortable explaining this to people, even to my close friends, we made up stock answers.

"Annie is blonde and big boned. She takes after my dad's family. I take after my mother's side," we would say. I wasn't ashamed of being adopted, but I did not want to look different to people outside the family. As far as I was concerned, adoption was family business and I did not want to keep explaining it to everyone.

My parents were loving and wonderful. They were truly a mom and dad sent from heaven. They were always there for me. We grew up on our dairy farm in upstate New York and had a wonderful family life. We had the usual sibling rivalries but my sister, my brother and myself were always close. We were a close family. After I completed college, I met Kevin, a handsome young man who later became my husband. Following better job opportunities, we moved to Cleveland, Ohio and eventually bought a home. My parents were the first to visit us, and Dad, a skilled carpenter, spent a lot of time fixing up our new home. No one ever had a better family life, and Kevin and I were planning to have our own family and be the same kind of loving parents to our children.

JEANNE: THE SEARCH

I began the search for my daughter in 1991 when I moved back to New York State from California. I was experiencing burn out from the years of stress caused by hospital nursing, and it was time for a change. I had just ended a relationship which I felt had no future. So what next? I began to realize that my parents weren't going to be around forever, and I wanted to spend more time with them. After all these years, I realized how much I missed my family. I also felt that something else, something really important, was missing in my life. I wasn't quite sure what it was...at least not consciously. Something powerful was pulling me back home, so I decided it was time to go back. Somehow it just felt like the right thing to do, and I was very excited about the new direction I was taking.

After being independent for twenty years, I moved in with my parents. They were very excited. I enrolled in school full time and began working on my bachelor's degree in nursing. But although I was happy about being home, it also triggered many of the old feelings of sadness. My coping mechanism of denying the fact that I had a child was suddenly beginning to crumble. I tried to live with it by staying busy with school and joining a local fitness club, working out every day.

My younger sister was very supportive. One day we were talking about a book we had read about family secrets. She told me she had watched an Oprah show about ALMA (Adoptee Liberation Movement Association), an adoption registry which also helped people search for children or parents. She said the name had caught her attention (my mother's first name being Alma) and also my first name. In order to avoid confusion, my parents had always called me Jeanne, which is really my middle name.

I began to think about the possibility of finding my daughter. It was now acceptable to talk about adoption. It was a common practice for people to search, and anyone could turn on the TV and watch children and parents being reunited. The culture which had stigmatized girls in my situation had finally changed to the point where I didn't have to hide my "secret" anymore. Even though it was painful, I realized that I was beginning to feel better. A reawakening was taking place.

I finally decided that I simply could not live my life any longer without knowing what had happened to my daughter. I needed to know if she was happy and healthy. I could no longer deny the fact that an important part of me was missing. I began my search by writing a letter to the Social Services department that had handled my daughter's adoption, and included a letter to be placed on file. It gave permission to give my daughter identifying information if she was, in fact, searching for me. I also requested non-identifying information.

My next step was to obtain my hospital records, along with my daughters hospital records. I remember reading them over and over again. I agonized over what to do. On one hand, I felt that I had no right to search after all this time. On the other hand, what if she needed me? What if she was desperately searching for me? I wanted to continue, but I didn't want to hurt anyone.

Several weeks later, I received a letter from the Social Services department's attorney stating that I was not entitled to any non-identifying information. He recommended signing up with the New York State Adoption Registry. I proceeded to fill out all the necessary papers and register. All I could do now was wait. If my daughter had also registered, there would be a match. In the meantime, I went to the local community college library to search through old newspapers. I thought I might find a birth and/or baptism announcement from the weeks following my daughter's birth, which would give me some clues. I also went to the Department of Records at the courthouse pretending to do a genealogy search. The staff tried to be helpful, and kept asking me a lot of questions about what I was looking for. This made me uncomfortable, and I didn't stay very long. I felt so close but yet so far away. I left feeling very discouraged because without a name, how could I possibly find her? She could be anywhere. But as discouraged as I was, I still knew that I couldn't give up. It made me angry that every door was closed, but it also made me more determined. I knew I had to find her. I finally signed up with two other adoption registries, ALMA and International Soundex.

By August of 1991, I was finishing a summer course at the community college. I was invited to a picnic, and it was there I met Paul. The picnic was at a private lake just outside Woodstock in the mountains. Just up the hill on top of the mountain was a breathtaking panoramic view of the Hudson River Valley, the Catskill Mountains, and the Ashokan Reservoir. Paul said he had a dream of someday building a house with a reservoir view like this. We seemed to hit it off right away. He lived in Woodstock, a place where I had also lived many years ago. We began to see each other on a regular basis. He loved the outdoors and was an avid cyclist. We rode bikes together, took hikes in the mountains, and spent hours in his rowboat on the reservoir. I had finally found my soul mate. After dating for several months, I moved in with him.

Paul is an audio engineer and owns an audio equipment rental business. He provides audio equipment to a number of major TV studios in New York City. In the fall of 1992, we took over his great- uncle's apartment in Manhattan. Paul began to work hard to nurture the growth of his business. He still clung to his dream of buying property, so after we saved enough money, we began searching for that "special spot." In 1993, we contacted the neighbor who lived just down the hill from the very same place where we had met, since we had talked to another neighbor at the party who told us they might have land for sale. Sure enough, they did. We made an appointment to meet with them. As soon as we saw the land we said, "Where do we sign?" We knew right away that this was exactly what we wanted. We realized a great deal of work had to be done, but the vision of our dream home sustained us.

Whenever we visited our apartment in New York City, there was always a considerable stack of mail waiting at the post office. One day, while sorting through the usual bundle of flyers and advertisements, I noticed a handwritten letter from California that bore a name I did not recognize. When I opened it and began reading, my heart began to pound. It was from a woman who was an ALMA volunteer, known as a "search buddy." She said that a long time ago they had received a letter from a sixteen-year-old girl named Michele from Connecticut with a birth date of June, 23, 1967. I had named my daughter Michele. Could this be my little girl searching for me?

As good as it sounded, we determined after several letter exchanges that this particular girl was not my daughter. I was extremely disappointed, since this was the first thread of evidence in twenty-five years concerning my daughter's whereabouts. Just as I thought I could see a light, I was once again thrown into the darkness. Nevertheless, the ALMA "support buddies" encouraged me to keep up the search and assured me that if I persisted, I would someday find my daughter. The "search buddies" would turn out to be the first of many wonderful people with whom I would come into contact on this long journey.

The inspiration from this experience led me to attend a meeting of ALMA at their New York City headquarters. After listening to one of their speakers, I met a woman who was also a birth mother. This was the first time I had a chance to speak to someone who was going through the same experience I was. I also met another "search buddy" who gave me a lot of tips on how to get started. The experience was a real eye-opener, because I suddenly realized there was a whole world out there full of people searching. It was very comforting to know that I was not alone.

Paul and I closed on our property in January of 1994. Happy and excited, we immediately began clearing trees to open up our view. We worked non-stop for the next year. Most days we were exhausted, but we just kept going. We had a lot of fun and made a good team. Neither of us had ever worked so hard, but it was extremely rewarding as we began to see some real progress. That year we also became engaged. We decided to wait and have the wedding at our "dream spot" after we finished the house.

Just as things were beginning to come together, my mother passed away suddenly on Christmas morning 1994. I was totally shocked and unprepared for the emotions that this event awakened in me. I became very depressed. My mother's death had triggered a feeling of loss like the one I felt so long ago when I lost my little girl. I began to really think about the mother--daughter relationship and how strong that relationship really is.

I realized how much I missed my mother. We had become very close. We had finally become friends and it was a great comfort to know she was there. Her death made me think even more about the fact that I had a daughter. Our recent closeness made me realize that if I had not come home, she could have died without us finding this intimacy. I thought about my dying without my own daughter ever knowing anything about me. I knew I had to find her.

One day after a long day of tree clearing, Paul and I were sitting at the picnic table admiring our beautiful view. I said, "Now I have almost everything... I have you and soon I'll have my dream home. But one thing is still missing. I don't have my daughter." I began to cry, and he promised me that we would find her and that one day she would come to visit us.

As my journey continued, I found a local support group for adoption triad (child, birth mother, adopted mother) members. I met a wonderful woman who had been adopted and was desperately searching for her birth mother. I was reminded that my daughter could be doing the same thing. This woman was extremely supportive and really helped me understand things from the adoptee's point of view.

I got the name of another company, called "Seekers of the Lost." I contacted them and gave them the small amount of information I had accumulated. They came up with a list of the names of all females in New York State with that birth date. There were over two hundred and fifty.

My next step was to begin a letter-writing campaign to all these girls. It was now the winter of 1996. Still preoccupied with our house project, there were long periods during which I didn't make much progress. I began to feel discouraged as I went down the list of names. I knew there was no guarantee that my daughter was there, and I didn't even know her name. I composed a form letter and began crossing names off the list as I began to send the letters out. Paul suggested setting up a separate telephone line with an answering machine in case I received calls.

Soon I began receiving letters from the girls I had contacted. Each one seemed to feel my pain and tried to reach out and comfort me, wishing me good luck with my search. I was very moved by the fact that these complete strangers were taking the time to respond and extend such kindness to me. Once again I was given an emotional boost just when I needed it the most. I felt as if I were getting closer to finding my daughter.

It was the summer of 1997 when I received a brochure in the mail with the class schedules from a local adult education program. One of the courses listed was entitled, "How to Find Anyone Anywhere." It was being taught by a former New York City police officer who was now a private investigator. I decided to call and find out more about it. The school gave me the instructor's telephone number, and I called to see if he could help. He was very honest. He told me adoptees were extremely difficult cases which were almost impossible to solve. He referred me to another local investigator who listened to my story and recommended a company known as World Wide Tracers who specialized in cases like mine. That company's main investigator was Pat Rutherford, and the local investigator was very confidant that if anyone could help me, Pat Rutherford could.

It had been six long years since I had begun my search. During that time, I would visit a church that was located around the corner from our city apartment. I loved to explore all the churches in the city and admire the beautiful, unique stained glass windows and the architecture. I don't remember the name of the church but I particularly liked it's windows. Being very close to our apartment, it became my own private escape from the noise and fast pace of the city. I always said a prayer and asked God to help me find my daughter. There was only one condition: it had to be a good thing for both of us. Each time before leaving, I would light a candle for my daughter, to keep the hope alive.

I called World Wide Tracers and spoke to a woman named Kyleen. She told me about Pat Rutherford and the service their company provided. I immediately said, "When can we start?" I gave them the information I had to initiate the investigation. I could feel the excitement building. I had finally found someone who might actually find my daughter! Kyleen reassured me that she would keep me informed of their progress.

Once again, all I could do was wait. I felt I was really getting close, and began working long hours on our house site with Paul in order to help the time pass more quickly.

Copy of Jeanne's search letter sent to over two hundred women.

March 11, 1997

Dear Karen

I am writing to you in hopes of finding my daughter who was born 6/23/67 at ******* hospital in Hudson, NY, (Columbia County) and was relinquished for adoption.

I contracted the services of an organization who searches for missing persons to do a computer search of their data bases. I was sent a list of names and addresses of all females registered to vote living in New York State with a birth date of 6/23/67. Of course, this is how I obtained your name and address.

If you think you are my daughter, please contact me at ********** (feel free to call collect). If you prefer to write, I have enclosed a self-addressed envelope.

I remain hopeful that I will soon be reunited with my daughter and thank you for your attention to this matter of great importance to me.

Best Regards,
Jean Biedrzycki
Shokan, NY 12481

My husband Kevin and I had just returned to Cleveland from our Florida vacation. The usual stack of mail was sitting on the dining room table, and I began sorting through it. One letter was from my mother. When I opened it, I discovered another letter inside addressed to me under my maiden name. Mom had simply placed the letter in the envelope and forwarded it to me, not knowing what it was. I did not recognize the name showing on the return address. Oh well, I thought, it could be a girl I knew in college with a new married name. When I opened the letter, I got the shock of my life.

It was a simple form letter. It started "Dear Karen," (the Dear was typewritten, the Karen was handwritten.) The handwritten parts (the name in the salutation and the signature, Jeanne Biedrzycki) were not original; the letter was obviously a photocopy. Other people must have received the same letter. I kept reading the part that said, "If you think you are my daughter, please call me".

I felt like I was cut in half. There was no doubt in my mind that I was the person she was describing and looking for. I was the baby girl born at the same hospital in Hudson, New York on June 23, 1967. It had to be me. Tears clogged my eyes and I began to sob. My husband could see I was visibly shaken, but even he could not comfort me. I had to speak to my parents. I ran to the phone and called them. Dad picked up the phone. As soon as he heard me speak, he knew something was wrong. I told him to get my mother on the extension, that I needed to talk to both of them right now.

My mother, Mary Lou, remembers her reaction when I called:

"Karen and her husband Kevin were both on the phone, so I knew that something must be wrong. Karen was crying while she was reading the letter to me. I knew how distressed

she was and I felt utterly helpless being five hundred miles away from her. I was ready to jump into the car or take the next train to Cleveland so I could comfort her. It was a very upsetting night, leaving a lot of questions unanswered, but after Karen calmed down we were sure she was in control and could handle it. The letter asked for a reply, so there was no great hurry. She would have time to think about it and compose herself."

Mom and Dad were as shocked as I was. They wanted to get on the next train out of New York, but I told them I could handle it. I just needed to know they were there for me. I asked what they thought my birth mother could want from me after thirty years. Mom said she didn't know, and began blaming herself for sending me the letter.

"You had no way of knowing what it was," I said. "I'm not upset over anything you've done."

After the initial shock had passed, and my parents were calm enough to talk it out, they assured me they would support any decision I made. I could sense the trepidation in their voices and knew they were deeply affected. As always, they were a tremendous comfort to me and I felt much better after talking to them. Later, they told me they called the pastor of their church that very evening and invited him to come to their house for guidance and prayer. My parents, very devout Christians, desperately wanted to make the right decision. They knew their daughter was going to need help getting through this situation, and they asked God to help them and me.

But my first reaction had been anger. Why was my birth mother looking for me now, after thirty years? What did she want? Who did she think she was, invading my life?

I needed time. I had to adjust to the idea. I thought about just ignoring the letter; I could just tuck it away and never deal with it again. After all, I had moved out of New

York and was married. This would surely make it difficult to locate me, and the whole thing would go away. But I could not get the letter out of my mind.

"If you think you are my daughter, please call me..."

The phrase kept leaping in and out of my head. I kept pulling the letter out from its hiding place and reading it.

I decided to take a different approach: I would do some reading on the subject of adoption. While I was growing up, I had never had a desire to read or inquire about it. So I made a trip to the local library and took home several books covering the adopted child's perspective, as well as those of the birth parents and the adoptive parents (known as the triad.) I tried to understand the social conditions of the 1960s into which I had been born. I tried to empathize with the young girls of that time, and imagine what it must have been like to have parents who told you what to do, as opposed to the many choices given young people today.

As I got more immersed in the subject, I began to feel my anger fade. In time, I began to understand the situation my birth mother must have found herself in. It also made me face and come to grips with the way I may have been conceived. I had always imagined that my birth mother wanted me, but was forced to give me up for adoption by her parents. It suddenly struck me that this might not have been the case. I was a little apprehensive about learning the truth. I read about young girls who were dumped after their boyfriends learned they were pregnant. I also read about children who were conceived out of rape. I didn't know how I would deal with the pain if this were the case. I prayed to God that this was not my situation, and to help me deal with whatever I found.

I began talking to some of my co-workers about the situation. Most shared the thought that I didn't owe this person a response.

"If you want to contact her, it should be on your terms," one advised.

Yes, of course, I thought to myself. Perhaps I will contact her, but it must be on my terms. I didn't feel was ready to make the next move. I would have to think about it and discuss it with my family at length. I had not really discussed my feelings with my husband and I felt I had to do that. Kevin's stepfather, Lewis had an adopted son from his first marriage, and I wanted to get his advice as well. I was simply "not ready." I needed to know more, and I needed more advice.

Books I had read were very helpful, but I hadn't ever spoken with another adoptee about the subject.

Although my brother was also adopted, he is mentally challenged and very introverted, so he was not someone with whom I could discuss my feelings. I didn't think it would help either of us to get his thoughts and feelings on the subject, notwithstanding the fact that we were siblings. Later, I learned from my mother that my brother was very upset about my birth mother contacting me, and he wanted to know if his birth mother was going to try to find him too. The subject matter was just too difficult for him to comprehend. I didn't want to upset him any further. My sister was also very supportive and I would like to have talked more at length with her, but it was difficult with her living so far away. She was able to get most of this from mom and dad since they lived in the same town back in New York.

Six months passed. Life got back to normal, and I felt I had the situation pretty much under control. One beautiful fall day in early October, I went to work as usual. But after I arrived at my office, my husband called. It was not unusual for Kevin to call me at work, but this time he sounded a bit strange. He told me our neighbor had come to our door the evening before, after I had already gone to bed for the evening. The neighbor said that he had received a strange telephone call from a private investigator in Texas who was trying to locate a Kevin and Karen Sweet at our address. My neighbor did not know our last name, but he told the investigator he would give the message to us. Wisely, Kevin, not wanting to upset me, did not give me the message immediately. Not knowing exactly what this was about, he decided to call the investigator first to find out.

Kevin found out the investigator was looking for me. He claimed New York State had hired him to find me because he had important medical information about my birth mother and her family, which needed to be passed on to me. Kevin tried to find out more, but that was all the investigator would tell him. He would only give me the information when I myself returned his call.

Kevin sensed how hard the news hit me. And indeed, tears filled my eyes as a new fear gripped me. Important medical information: what could be so bad that the State of New York, which was supposed to protect my adoptive records, would help an investigator find me? A co-worker, seeing my distress, asked me if I was all right. I couldn't answer him. He offered to drive me home, but I refused. I was still crying as I walked to my car. I'd thought I had the situation under control. I'd thought I would be the one to make the first move. Now I was being forced to act.

I was still not over my fear when I arrived home. I stared at the number on the paper, yet could not bring myself to call. I laid down on the bed and began crying again. Finally, I began to gain control; I do not know where I got the courage, but I finally managed to make the call.

The private investigator's name was Pat Rutherford. He began telling me the medical information he had from my birth family. There was a history of cancer in the family. My birth mother's mother had had breast and cervical cancer, confirming my worst fears. He then began volunteering more information than he was supposed to, saying that he had spoken with my birth mother several times and that there had not been a day when she hadn't been searching for me. He asked if she could call me. I said, "No."

I couldn't keep the tears from flowing throughout the conversation, and at times had a difficult time even getting words out. But Mr. Rutherford was sensitive, caring, and patient. He shared with me the fact that he too had adopted children, and could understand my situation. It was very reassuring. All the way from Texas his voice was having a calming effect on me. In the midst of my fear and confusion, I was also experiencing something I had never felt before about this situation: curiosity.

Mr. Rutherford began asking me questions about how I was raised, whether I had other siblings, etc. I told him I had been adopted by wonderful, loving parents, that I had an adopted brother, and that my younger sister was my parent's biological child. I told him I had grown up on a dairy farm. He told me that my natural mother had also grown up on a dairy farm.

In between his description of his own adopted children, I related the circumstances of my childhood. It had been happy, with a large extended family, which consisted of many cousins, all of whom had accepted my brother and I as just part of the family. I made it clear that I never had a desire to search for my natural parents because I had grown up in such a secure and loving home. I had never really dwelt upon what adoption actually meant, and I had never felt that I was loved less because I wasn't my parent's natural child. Adoption was just a word to me. "I already have a mother," I told him.

Knowing that I was unwilling to call my birth mother or give out my unlisted telephone number, Mr. Rutherford did give me her name, number and address and asked me to consider writing to her. Her name was Jeanne. I already knew her name from the form letter but I questioned Mr. Rutherford further and found out that Jeanne had never married, and had no other children. Mr Rutherford told me she felt that if she ever did get married, it would have to be for the "right reasons." She had been living with her boyfriend/fiancé for the last seven years and they were building a home. It was her dream that I would be at their wedding. I thanked Mr. Rutherford for the information and told him I would have to think about this. He asked if it would be alright for Jeanne to write to me and I agreed.

I took the form letter out again. I stared at the phrase, "If you think you are my daughter, please call me...". Suddenly it was no longer a form letter. This statement was coming from a person, Jeanne. She had a name. I could feel her pain and emptiness as I pondered Mr. Rutherford's words. He said she had never married or had any other children; I thought of my own family and could feel the sadness she must have felt being alone for so long. Jeanne was no longer a letter I could tuck away in a drawer and ignore. She had become a person with fears and emotions, with whom I was tied.

I immediately called my parents and shared the news with them. They were very supportive and assured me they would stand behind me no matter what decision I made. I was an adult and had to deal with this myself, but they would always love me no matter what. I asked them not to tell my sister and brother right away. I needed more time to decide what I would do. I knew pursuing contact would affect my entire family. I wanted to make the right decision. I wanted to be sure.

My mother remembers how she felt when that phone call arrived:

"When Karen called me the second time and told me about the private investigator, our world was turned upside down. This time there was no choice. Our lives had been invaded by someone unknown to us. I remember feeling very insecure, wondering what this woman wanted. If it was medical information, as we were being told, why now? Then I thought, what would be a good time for news like that?

Medical information could be anything and, as a nurse, I knew the kind of concern that cancer could be in a family history . Mixed with that weight was my concern about my position of being a mother. Was I going to be replaced as a mother? Did this woman have another motive as well, other than trying to get to know Karen? I did a lot of crying and thought that no one really understood what I was feeling; after all, no one else was the one being replaced. I was also troubled that this woman had our address. I wondered if she had passed by our home and if we had ever met. How much did she know about us?

Of course, I would never let Karen know about these feelings. She was an adult and I knew she could handle it. We would be there to support her. I had always told Karen that when she was ready to find her biological mother, we would gladly help her. I thought it would be exciting and interesting. But now that the reality of it was here, I felt completely different about it. My daughter was distressed and now it seemed more like a nightmare."

MY DAUGHTER HAS BEEN FOUND!

About three months had passed since I'd last talked to World Wide Tracers. One day I returned to the house and checked the answering machine. There was a message waiting for me from Kyleen. They had found my daughter! I remember my first thought was "Thank God she is alive and well." I think I must have been in shock, because it took me a while to respond. I remember I went back over to the house site, which was right next door to tell Paul the good news. I was wandering about feeling dazed, still disbelieving it. So many thoughts were going through my head...and suddenly I was thrown back in time. I was that sixteen-year-old mother again and I was picturing this baby, my baby. I had visions of baby clothes. But ...she wasn't a baby anymore. She was all grown up...thirty years old. It was too much to fathom. All this was impossible to imagine because in my mind she had never really grown up. She was always my little girl.

When I finally got it together and called Kyleen, she informed me that they had located my daughter, told me her name, and that she had already received my form letter. That meant she already had my name and address. She had been very shocked and reluctant to call me, but finally agreed to my writing her. I was thrilled beyond belief. After nearly thirty years, my search was finally over. But, it turned out to be just the beginning: The start of another search, the search to find the missing pieces, was still ahead for me. My daughter had also given Mr. Rutherford permission for me to write to her.

The Letters

I began to think about the first letter I would write to Karen. I agonized over choosing the right words. This was going to be the first impression she would have of me as a person, so I knew it had to be right. It was like walking on eggshells. Where did I begin? As anxious as I was to finish the letter and get it mailed, I did not want to make a mistake. I was horrified at the prospect of being rejected, so I rewrote it many times, making sure I wasn't being presumptuous. I certainly did not want to offend her adoptive parents or upset her family.

I kept reading the letter over, wondering if it was all right. Finally I reached the point where I couldn't read it again; what I wrote would have to do. When I reached the end, I paused over how to close. I decided to use the words "Your other mother," hoping this would convey my feelings and not offend Karen. I thought of signing just my name, Jeanne, but my feelings were too strong. In my mind she was still my daughter, and I would have to take the chance. Rejected or not, Karen had to know how I felt. All I could do was send it and have faith that God had guided me.

October 11, 1997

Dear Karen,

I never really believed in miracles until now, but I truly believe that my prayers have been answered! This is the happiest day of my life because I have found my "little girl" and she is happy and healthy. What more could I have asked for? I am so thankful to know that your adoptive parents took such wonderful care of you and provided you with a happy childhood. I know that you must love them very much.

I have to tell you that it absolutely broke my heart when you were taken away from me. You must understand that I was only sixteen years old and my parents did what they thought was best for me as well as their grandchild, and I really had no choice in the matter. (In other words, it was done out of love.) You also have to keep in mind that it was a different era. It was a small town and people were much less accepting of this situation than they are today.

There is so much I would like to talk about, but for now I'll tell you a little about my life and your "other family." First of all, I grew up on a dairy farm in Elizaville, NY. I went to school at Germantown Central and graduated in 1968. In 1971, I graduated from the RN nursing program at Columbia Memorial. My first job was at a hospital in Kingston, NY in the ICU-CCU Dept. I moved to Florida in 1975 where I spent the next 10 years. I continued to work in hospital nursing during this time.

In 1985 I moved to San Diego, CA and left there in 1987 to move up to Santa Cruz. I really enjoyed California and the western United States. But this time I was beginning to tire of hospital nursing, which had become very stressful. So I began taking classes at the community college with the idea that I would get my bachelor's degree in nursing.

In 1991 I moved back to NY to finish up my BSN degree at New Paltz, and graduated in 1994. During this time I had had several long term relationships, but never married and had no other children. I finally met the most wonderful man during the summer of 1991 when I moved back to NY. His name is Paul Cohen. He is the light of my life and we are very happy together. Paul has a very successful business "Paul Cohen Audio Services." He works in television production and provides sound equipment for several major TV shows in New York City. We maintain an apartment in Manhattan, since all of Paul's clients are in the city. In 1994 we bought 11 acres of land just outside of Woodstock with a beautiful view of the Ashokan Reservoir and Catskill Mountains. We have spent the past three years clearing trees to open up the view and putting in the driveway. Right now we are in the process of building our "dream home." All of the planning and hard work has paid off, and so far we are very pleased and excited with the results. They are finishing up the roof now and we hope to have it enclosed by Thanksgiving. We will take our time finishing the inside, and will probably move in by next summer or fall.

In our spare time Paul and I enjoy taking walks. Yesterday we took a hike up the mountain with our neighbors and their little girl. We are real nature lovers and spend a lot of time outdoors working at our property,

watching the animals (birds, deer, turkeys, etc.) and watching the sunrise and sunsets over the mountains.
My immediate family consists of my two sisters, Kay, 5 yrs. younger, and Linda, 5 yrs. older. Kay has four girls, ages twelve to eighteen, Glorianne, Kathleen, Alana, and Shannon. Linda has one daughter, Debbie age, age twenty-nine, who is married and has two children. Kay is also a nurse and runs the farm. She raises thoroughbred race horses. I think that she has about twenty-five to thirty horses at present.

Linda is a ward secretary at the hospital. My dad's name is Lee. He is 82 and still does all the tractor work on the farm. They just finished baling the last of the hay last week. Unfortunately, my mother is no longer with us. She died in 1994 of a very sudden hear attack. She was very active and apparently healthy up until the day before she died.

Of course I could go on forever, but I want to get this letter off to you. The most important message that I want to convey to you right now is that this is all positive and good. I hope that it will help to provide closure and peace of mind for both of us. You are my daughter and I love you very much. My only wish is for you to be happy.

I'm sure that you must know by now how anxious I am to hear from you. I want to know all about your life, your family, and the things you enjoy doing. That would make me very happy!
Much Love,
Your other mother Jeanne
P.S. The greatest gift that I could receive would be to hear the sound of your voice.

KAREN: ANSWERING THE LETTER

I came home from work one day and checked the mail. In the myriad of advertising flyers, bills, and envelopes, one letter almost jumped out of the stack. The return address told me it was Jeanne. I threw the other mail aside and opened it. I felt my heart ache as I read. Buried in the facts about family and work history was a phrase that I kept reading over and over:

"I have to tell you that it absolutely broke my heart when you were taken away from me."

The phrase was followed by the disclosure of the fact that I was given up for adoption because the family thought it was the right thing to do for a sixteen-year-old mother. I began to understand and I could feel what this woman had gone through.

I knew I could not ignore her letter. I was not ready for her to hear the sound of my voice, but I decided to write back. I collected my thoughts and began to compose a letter to my birth mother. But what do you write to a stranger who isn't really a stranger? After all, she did conceive me, carry me for nine months, and give birth to me. Yet we never "met." I needed to express both curiosity and caution in one letter. My emotions were running high as I groped for the words that would express my feelings.

October 24, 1997

Dear Jeanne,

I must start by saying that I never really thought that you would ever come looking for me, so I am sure you can understand that when I received the first form letter back in April it was completely shocking and emotionally overwhelming.

I had a good idea back then that you were my natural mother, but I wasn't really sure what to do. I decided to take a little time to explore my feelings. I needed to overcome the questions I kept asking myself: Why now? What does this person want? Do I even want to be found? During that time, I talked to my parents and did a lot of reading. I tried to get a better understanding of how things were for you back then. The reading helped me deal with my feelings and gave me some insight into the problem.

I had always convinced myself that you, my biological mother, had had no choice but to give me up. You must have been forced into it. This fantasy helped me deal with the problem of accepting why I was given up.

I grew up in Stuyvesant, NY. My parents named me Karen Eileen. I have an older adopted brother, David, who is mentally challenged, and a younger sister, Annie, who is my parent's biological daughter. I also grew up on a dairy farm and spent a great deal of time playing with my cousins. I was in 4-H, and was a Brownie and a Girl Scout. I took piano lessons but didn't stick with it (although I wish I had). My first job was working for a local McDonalds, where I stayed four years. I was a freshman cheerleader in high school and would describe myself as an average student. I graduated on my birthday in 1985 and attended a small private College in Longmeadow, MA, majoring in retail management, and graduated in 1987.

My first real job was as a sales coordinator for a small company and later I worked for an energy consulting firm. I now work for a large bank as an AVP in our mutual funds department. Being a Key Accounts Manager is a job I really enjoy. I wound up moving to Cleveland after the bank division I work for moved here three years ago.

My husband, Kevin, and I love Cleveland a lot but miss our families back in New York. We have a very happy yet hectic life. We are both in school right now so things are very busy.

Kevin and I met in February of 1992. Some of my college friends had come to visit me and we decided to go out. The MC at the nightclub called for a Sadie Hawkins dance, and I asked Kevin to dance. The rest is history. We got married on September 10th of 1994 and moved to Cleveland in January of 1995, with our Jack Russell terrier, Hannah. We rented for six months, then purchased our first home and a second dog, MacKenzie. We love our puppies very much. We have a great circle of friends, some of whom came from Albany like we did, and some of whom we have met here. In addition to that, one of our family members is always visiting.

About you and me? I'm not really sure how things are supposed to work. I guess I am wondering what you expect now after thirty years. I'm showing my cautious side.

I probably have more questions now than I ever had growing up. Probably because I grew up in such a secure family, I always accepted my adoption and never really questioned the why and the how.

But now all of sudden I have this whole other family and it's hard to digest all of this. My husband has been extremely supportive and my parents have been very understanding. So, I guess I am wondering, what is next?

I suppose we should start by continuing to write. I am very curious about the severity of your mother's breast and cervical cancer... that scares me a bit. I'd like to know as much as possible so I can update my family history with my doctor. I'd also like to share my other questions with you. I hope you are OK with this for now.

Jeanne, please try to understand why I was angry with this at first. But I have tried to see the situation from your side and I'm glad to know I was wanted. This is how I've accepted it. I tell myself, "God sent me to my parents through you," just like my card says: "You are a special person in my life, after all you gave me life."

Karen

P.S. Please bear with me as we go through this. I'm not sure how or what to do next.

KAREN: SENDING THE LETTER

I decided to mail the letter with a card and included some pictures. I searched for a card with the right words and placed the letter inside. My feelings were still very guarded and I re-read the letter, convinced that it was articulating the right feeling of caution. I still felt confused about what the next step should be.

Mixed with this feeling of caution was the feeling of relief. I had always had a fantasy about the circumstances of my birth: I was conceived out of love, and my birth mother must have been forced to give me up. It was a defense mechanism I used in order to live with the circumstances. Having this confirmed filled in a huge gap in my life. For this I was grateful. It would have been much tougher to deal with any other circumstances.

November 9, 1997

Dear Karen,

On Monday, I went to the post office to check the mail with hopes of having a letter from you waiting in my box. Sure enough, there it was! My heart started pounding (literally). When I opened it and saw the pictures. I couldn't believe my eyes! My dreams had finally come true. I was looking at my beautiful daughter. Words cannot describe how happy I felt. It was also a very spiritual moment, looking at you and seeing so much of myself.

I spent a long time looking at the pictures over and over again. I thought to myself how proud your parents must be. I especially enjoyed seeing the pictures of your family. I could tell by their eyes and the smiles on their faces what good people they must be.

Thank you so much for the beautiful card. The picture of the garden path is beautiful. My dream is that someday we could walk down such a path together, enjoying all the beauty that surrounds us. I feel as if we have been given a wonderful gift, the opportunity to get to know each other. It is a new chapter in our lives, one that we can create and share together. I hope it can be a happy one. I'd like to know what you think. In any case, there is no pressure or expectations about anything right now. We're just sharing thoughts and trying to feel our way together, OK?

I think Paul was almost as excited as I was. He has been so sweet and supportive during this whole thing. Anyway, he can't get over how much we look alike! He is very optimistic about everything. He has some thoughts that he wants to share with you and is in the process of composing a letter.

Your letter helped me understand how difficult this must be for you. I'm so glad you have a wonderful support system as well. I know how much it means. I am very thankful you no longer feel angry. I was very touched by the final thoughts you expressed in your letter, a beautiful way of looking at it. I can tell you are intelligent, sensitive, and a loving person able to see the bright side of a difficult situation and make the most of it.

I'll close on this note; the way I look at it now is that we have been guided back to each other for an important reason and it is up to us to discover it.

Please keep the letters and pictures coming.

Love,
Jeanne

JEANNE

I was thrilled and excited to read the letter from Karen. The picture album was very helpful. It helped me put things into perspective. Until now, I could not think of Karen as having grown up. But I couldn't help noticing the striking resemblance we had at certain ages. Anyone comparing our pictures could see that this was my daughter. I had to recapture thirty years in a few minutes.

I also began to feel a certain anger. I realized just how much I had lost. Thirty years I could never get back. I had to be careful that the anger did not consume me. It began to temper when I looked at the pictures again. I began etching the striking resemblance into my mind. No one could ever take that away from me. They could take my baby away, but not the resemblance. It was all I had. It would have to do for now.

KAREN

I was busy with the holidays. First, Kevin's mother and stepfather visited the weekend before Thanksgiving. On Thanksgiving, Kevin's father, stepmother, and sister arrived. Finally, I decided to answer Jeanne's letter. It seemed that Jeanne liked the cards I picked out. I composed a new letter and placed it inside the card. On the card itself, I explained why I was so late in answering and described some of the family affairs we were holding during the holidays. I thanked her for her beautiful letter. As curious as I was to learn about my birth mother, I was still fearful about the medical information that I was supposed to receive. I learned later that important as the cancer information was, the investigator had emphasized it in order to get the court records opened. Nevertheless, the information was important and I had a right to know. The letter inside the card is shown below.

December 4, 1997

Dear Jeanne,

I have to be honest. I was filled with a "warmness" that is hard to describe. I guess up until this point I still was a little apprehensive.

After I received you letter, I called my mom to share with her your warm sentiments. She was very happy for me! Both my parents have been extremely supportive.

I guess I would like to continue to get to know each other better by continuing to write. For now this is "comfortable" for me. Although I do share your letters with Kevin, it is really something between you and me.

My thoughts are that we can explore our feelings and learn more about each other's lives. I also, at some point in the future, would like to have answers to questions I have had for a long, long time. This, however, would be more appropriate in person and right now, I'm not ready to have those answered just yet.

Some of my questions have been answered just by your actions. I can't tell you how important it was to me to know just how wanted I was even though the circumstances did not allow it.

I do have questions about the breast and cervical cancer and on the family history. I have been worried! Until now I had to answer "NO" to those types of questions my family doctor would ask. Now that I can answer "YES," I need to understand the severity. I have heard reports that women who have a family history should start getting checked about ten years earlier than normal. I'm going to the OB-GYN tomorrow and want to start discussing this topic with him. Although I've never had any problems, I want to be cautious.

Here is a little more about myself. Although I work for a bank, I have never worked in a branch. My position was in the financial services brokerage arm that provides investments in downtown Albany. I still work for the same bank, but currently in the mutual fund department in their Cleveland office.

In regards to my education, I started back to school for my undergraduate degree about a year and a half ago. I attend a local college and have six classes left and hope to be finished by next summer. I took time off after my associates degree to obtain several securities licenses needed for my job.

Kevin is always telling me that I have a "plan" or "goal" that I set for myself... and that I take on too much. I guess I find it very rewarding. I would like to go on for my MBA, but we really want to start thinking about starting a family. I want to enjoy my pregnancy and not have the added stress of school. So for now we are waiting to finish school.

I've enclosed more pictures. We don't have a fax machine, but we do have e-mail. Do you have e-mail? I like getting e-mail and exploring the Internet, and perhaps this could be a better way for us to communicate.

Questions for you:

Where do you work now and what do you do?
Do you live in the city during the week also?
What is your favorite color, season?
What religion are you?
Do you have any animals?

I look forward to your next letter or e-mail. I hope you enjoy the holidays.

Take care,

Karen

KAREN

I could tell my feelings were beginning to change. Reading Jeanne's letters made me realize that she was a good person. Yes, a good person who had been dealt a severe blow in her early life. I tried to put myself in her place, tried to feel her pain. I imagined what it must have been like for her. I also knew that her circumstances came about in different times. I think that was the most difficult part for me to understand. I could feel myself softening as I pondered her situation and read her letters.

December 12, 1997

Dear Karen,

Once again your lovely card, photos, and letter brought tears of joy to my eyes! I must admit that I was becoming a bit concerned because I hadn't heard from you. It sounds like you have really had your hands full, and I can understand the delay.

I can definitely relate to your situation. Working and going to school is not easy. I think that your idea of e-mailing each other is great! It would make it much easier to stay in touch. It would be a lot faster since it takes four to five days for our letters to reach each other.

It is also much easier for me to organize my thoughts on the computer. My computer experience is limited to word processing and the Quicken program I use for Paul's business. Right now we have a laptop computer, but Paul has wanted a desktop for some new Internet audio programs. We are both very curious about all of that. I took a one-day course, and that is the extent of my knowledge on the subject. It looked fascinating and I think that the timing is definitely right. I told Paul that he could go ahead and shop around for a new desktop computer, so he is very happy. I told him he has you to thank!

In response to your question, "Where do I work?," when I started back to school in 1991 I took a part-time private duty position on two cases that my sister Kay was also working on. I eventually gave up one case when more hours opened up on the other. I take care of a 44 year old man who is a quadriplegic. He is a really nice fellow. He is always polite and has a good attitude and sense of humor. I am amazed by the fact that he copes so well with his situation. He has been an inspiration to me. Whenever I think that I have a problem, I think of him and it helps put things into perspective. What started as a temporary job has lasted for 7 years. I enjoy the fact that I am my own boss, and the money and hours are also very good. It works well with Paul's crazy schedule. It allows me the flexibility of going to the city with him, at least part of the time.

Your next question, "My favorite colors?" Again, another tough question. I can tell you what I don't care for: yellow and orange (except at Halloween). If I had to choose, I guess it would be maroon, grape, or lavender. If I look at my wardrobe I see a lot of navy, black, maroon, and white.

"What is my favorite season?" It has always been fall. It is the season I missed the most when I lived in Florida and California, because nothing else compares to the beauty of the New England fall foliage. I enjoy all of the Halloween decorations, pumpkin carving, apple cider, and yard work outside with Paul.

I am a Protestant, specifically Dutch Reformed. I attended Sunday school every week during my childhood years and went to vacation Bible school. I do not attend church now on a regular basis.

I hope this will give you a better window into my world. I have started working on the family medical history. I'd like to try and do that on the computer so you have a good copy.

I have to get ready for work. We just got about 6" of snow! I love reading your letters because it makes me feel close to you! So I look forward to your next letter and will keep you in my thoughts. Much Love,
Jeanne

Ironically, Jeanne was a nurse just like my mother. We seem to have had many things in common. Brought up on a farm, loved the fall of the year, and it seemed as though we were both interested in crafts. Jeanne had many similarities to my own mother, I thought.

December 15, 1997

Dear Jeanne,

I hope you are enjoying the holiday season. I certainly have been. Thank you for the Christmas CD, it was a nice surprise. I have been listening to it in the car.

Your last letter left me feeling like I know more about you, so thank you for sharing that with me. It sounds like you have the best of both worlds; all the cultural aspects of New York City and the peace and scenery of upstate NY.

Cleveland on a smaller scale actually offers both although it has the lake, but no mountain views. This has been a fun year in Cleveland. The city has really been in the spotlight.

Our community offers a lot to do. We have a big metro park system where we walk the dogs, go roller-balding, and launch our Jet Ski. Our friends have a boat, so we often go out together. This past summer I actually got a tan without going on vacation. We also enjoy baseball. The Indians had a great year and the playoff game had the city and fans aglow.

We love having friends over. During the winter we shoot darts in our basement, play music, and eat. There is a group of seven of us that moved from Albany at the same time and we have become very close. We've become each other's family.

Glad to hear that you are going to get a computer. I think that you will really like it. I get on the Internet for about an hour every night. There is so much to look at and play with.

I guess I have more questions:

Do you have any Christmas family traditions?
What are you doing for the holidays?

I have been thinking a lot about the New Year and maybe we could talk about what it could bring. I have a good feeling about 1998! Hope you enjoy the little gift. I am looking forward to your next letter.

Karen

December 19, 1997

Dear Karen,

I received your package several days before Christmas. Thank you for the letter and photos. In response to your questions about holiday traditions for the past few years our immediate family has gathered together at my sister Linda's house on Christmas Eve to open our gifts together.

Thank you for the handmade Christmas ornament. I will be putting it on the tree every year and each time I hang it I will think of you. So you see, it is perfect, as I know it is a gift from the heart and that means more to me than you could imagine. I also wore the pin on Christmas and continued to wear it and feel your presence with me all day long. This definitely brought smiles into my Christmas, thank you!

You mentioned that you had a good feeling about 1998. I also feel extremely optimistic and feel many good things will come in the New Year. So, I would love to "talk" and hear your thoughts whenever you are ready to share your ideas.

In the meantime, I like all of your questions. I've enjoyed answering them because I think that it is a good way to find out "who I am." All of these little things say a lot about me and my personality. So I guess it would help me for you to answer some of the same questions. How tall are you? What size do you wear? What hobbies do you have?

I also hope that you had a great holiday and enjoyed your visit with your family and friends. I'll be anxious to hear all about it.

Much love,

Jeanne

P.S. Could you please send me a hand print with your next letter? Just trace it on a piece of paper.

KAREN

It was a beautiful letter. I felt my heart ache when I read the Post Script again. It struck me that this is what mothers get their children to do when they are young. Jeanne, of course, never knew me when I was young, but she still yearned for that precious artifact of childhood: a hand print. It was all she could settle for. The maternal instinct. I traced my hand print on a piece of note paper and sent it with my next letter.

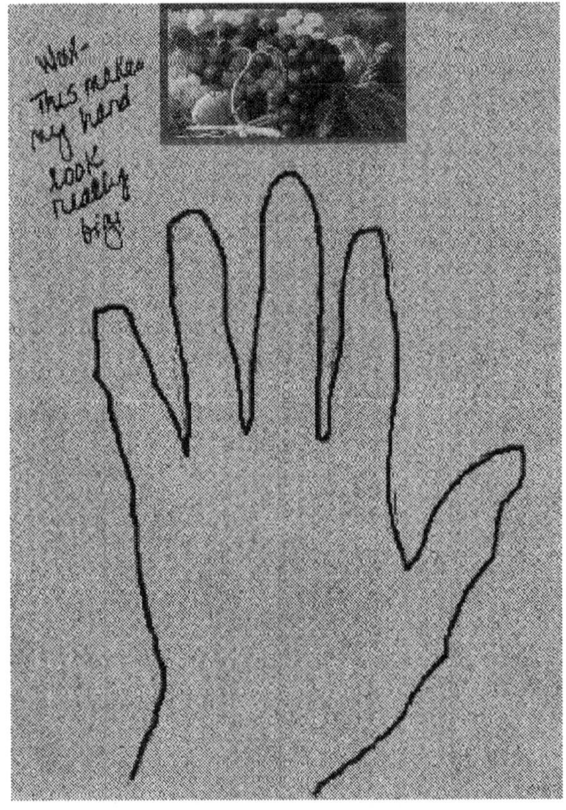

JEANNE

I must admit that I looked at the hand print before I read the letter. I just had to place my own hand on it. It was a perfect match! Excitement welled up in me; I felt like I was touching my daughter. As I looked down at my hand, tears of sheer happiness obliterated my hand and the tracing. When I wrote back, I could hardly contain myself.

KAREN

I realized that I had a decision to make. At some point in time, I would have to set up a meeting with Jeanne. I noticed that she never mentioned this, so I thought she was probably leaving the decision up to me. But I was not ready. The caution I felt was still more powerful than the sentiment I was feeling. I had my own parents to think about, and I would not hurt their feelings for anything in the world.

January 5, 1998

Dear Jeanne,

Happy New Year! It sounds like you had a nice holiday with friends and family. To me that is what the holiday is all about. I am so thankful for the many blessings of the season.

Thank you so much for our gifts. The chimes are hanging in the kitchen until spring and I love the little heart ornament. I am going to keep it out year round.

My week back in NY went quickly. I spent most of my trip at my parents. My dad had surgery, so I had to take him to the doctor and hospital. Another day was spent at pre-school with my niece and nephew awaiting the arrival of Santa. Kevin drove home to Schenectady on Christmas Eve, so after church I drove up to meet him at my in-laws. Christmas Day was spent with both sets of his parents. Then on Friday we visited friends and went back to my parent's to exchange gifts with the rest of my family. We returned to Cleveland and spent New Year's Eve with a group of friends at some local pubs near our home in Lakewood.

I am glad you liked your card and gifts. This is my third year making Christmas cards. I did also make the tree ornament, but bought the pin at a craft fair. I like making gifts people appreciate.

Now to answer some of your questions. Regarding religion, I was raised Lutheran and was baptized, confirmed, and married in the Lutheran church. My mom is the organist at our church, a position she has held over 20 years. Kevin is Methodist, and when we moved to Ohio we joined a local Methodist Church. My favorite colors include red and royal blue; however, my wardrobe has a lot of brown and tan the basics. My work suits are navy, brown and black. I am a size 4 petite and stand 5'4" tall. I always have to try everything on. Regarding music, I don't really follow any artist or have a favorite group. I like a variety of music. Kevin and I like to dance, so the top twenty type of dance music is what we enjoy. I like instrumentalists like Kenny G and some classical music like the traditional favorites of Tchaikovsky. We had a harpist at our wedding and she was great. This Christmas I bought myself a harp Christmas cassette. I also like Celtic music.

Hobbies? Well, restoring old trunks is a favorite. Kevin and I also have a Jet Ski, so we spend a lot of time on the lake in the summer and we love to take walks to watch the sun set on Lake Erie. Kevin keeps asking me when you are getting your computer. I guess he is anxious for us to get online as well.

Take Care,
Karen

January 20, 1998

Dear Karen,

I was very happy when I peeked into my post office box and found your letter waiting for me! I called Paul at the shop to let him know. He is so cute he gets just as excited as I do! (That's why I love him so much). Anyway, your letters have become a real highlight for both of us.

Thank you for the Christmas photos. I love all of your decorations. It sounds like you really have a lot of fun, which is great. I feel like I can visualize your world much better now. It is like putting a puzzle together, slowly gathering the pieces. The photos really help. I've started a "Karen album" and have lots of pages to fill.

Your letter sounded very happy and I was glad to hear all of your news and your hobbies. We too enjoy going to craft shows as well. I have been keeping my eyes open for interesting art classes. Maybe in my old age I'll become an artist, as I am surrounded by so much beauty on the mountain.

I meant to tell you in my last letter that I was happy to hear you and Kevin were planning to start a family soon. I think that it would be wise from a medical standpoint not to wait too much longer. I did not experience any problems during my pregnancy with you, but there was an RH incompatibility. I'm RH negative and you are O positive. Anyway, I don't know if you are aware of the fact that you had a blood transfusion when you were born. Your doctor can probably explain it better than I can. I don't think that it is something to worry about. Needless to say, it would be very special for me to have the opportunity to watch your children grow up and share in that wonderful experience.

Well, guess what! UPS delivered our new computer today! So it won't be long until we're online together. I'm really excited. I'll still enjoy the letter writing because it is more personal; however, it is time-consuming. This will speed things up and make it a lot easier to stay in touch. Look for messages from me in your email.

Much love to you and Kevin too!
Jeanne

A "Karen album." Something to add to the hand print. I thought perhaps I should send her more copies of my baby pictures to add to that album. I would have to think about that.

The computer had arrived. Now we could communicate instantly.

I thought about my parents. I did not want to lose sight of the fact that I needed to keep in touch with them. They did not have a computer, and I wanted them to be kept informed. I decided that I would have to telephone them more often. They must have felt a little threatened, but they never showed it. It was important to keep them totally involved, not only for their sake but for mine. I needed to be able to talk openly with them about everything and share feelings. I felt I could never get through this without them.

The E-Mails

E-mails started a new phase of our relationship. Old fashioned letter writing had served its purpose. I needed to take things slowly, and the letter writing had been perfect. It gave me time to think about things between responses, and Jeanne also admitted that it gave her time to pause and think as well. As much as she would have liked for it to move at a faster pace, she realized that I was not ready. The slower tempo and contemplative nature of letter writing helped melt the ice and keep our emotions under control. But now we were ready for the next step in our relationship.

I was now seeing things in a different light and felt a great deal more at ease talking to Jeanne. Jeanne had my e-mail address and wrote just as soon as her computer was up and running. There was not much in her first e-mail, which let me know that she was online. I composed my first e-mail to her.

From: Ksweet1072@aol.com
Sent: Sunday, January 25,1998 11:07 am
To: Jeanneb1@IBM.Net
Subject: A Nice Sunday Morning Surprise

Good Morning!

I received your message a little while ago. I was actually thinking about you yesterday and was going to write you a card today because I hadn't heard from you.

Well, now that you are hooked up we can send messages more frequently. Actually, we sometimes get so busy that we don't check everyday, but for some reason I thought I would check this morning to see what we had, and I was happy to get your message.

I have been thinking more about us. I feel really good with the pace we are at and that we are slowly getting to know each other. Yesterday I went to the library and took a book out called Birth Bond, Reunions of Birth Parents, and Adult Adoptees. I want to take some time and read it. I know no book will have all of the answers on moving ahead, but it is something I need to do for myself at this stage.

I have a question that I have been thinking about for a few weeks. What does your dad think of all of this? Does he say much? Being my maternal grandfather, I am curious.

I'm excited about your new computer. You will absolutely love it! I have to tell myself to stay on for only an hour at a time or I would stay all day.

Hope to hear from you soon.

Take care, Karen

I printed this e-mail and read it over again before I sent it. I had no reservations about asking a personal question about her father's feelings and thinking of him as my maternal grandfather. I composed another message.

From: Ksweet1072@aol.com
Sent: Monday, January 26, 1998, 4:01pm
To: Jeanneb1@IBM.net
Subject: Quick Note

Hi, Just a quick note to tell you I received your e-mail last night and I received your letter today.

I too get very excited to hear from you as well. I can't seem to read your letters fast enough for Kevin, as he anxiously waits to read them too. I am saving all of our correspondence as well.

Anyway, I have to run, I have a big test tonight. I'll respond to your letter later.

Karen

KAREN:

I began to see my anger and shock being replaced with curiosity and excitement. Yet there was still the ghost of caution in my heart. I still felt the need to absorb all this. I had come a long way, but still had a long way to go. I responded to Jeanne's e-mail but not hastily. I still needed time to think about them after I read them. I was not completely out of the letter-writing mode.

The next e-mail I received was from Paul.

From: PCCohen@IBM.net
Date: Tuesday, January 27, 1998 4:09 pm EST
To: Ksweet1072@aol.com
Subject: Hello from Paul

Karen & Kevin,

I have enjoyed having Jeanne share your letters with me. I prayed for a long time that she would find you, and that life for you has been good.

Somehow I feel it is important for me to introduce myself and paint a picture of what our life here in Shokan is like.

I grew up in New Haven, CT and moved to Woodstock after finishing high school when I was seventeen. I worked on the road as an audio engineer touring with various bands until 1980. I then started freelancing, doing television production in Manhattan. In 1985 I built an 1,800-square-foot shop in Saugerties as the center of activities for my audio business. I met Jeanne six years ago. We lived in a small house in Bearsville that

I was renting, then moved to Shokan a year ago. In 1991, we took over my great-uncle's apartment in Manhattan on the East Side, as a place for us to stay when I'm working in the city.

Four years ago we bought 11 acres of property, where the two of us have cut hundreds of trees, pulled 300 stumps, drilled and blasted 300 holes, moved many hundreds of dump truck loads of shale and dirt, and burned brush on 100+ days. We also created a driveway, installed temporary power, and reshaped a four-acre shale quarry. This past winter we refined plans for our new house with our contractor and through this fall have gotten the structure shelled up. We are likely to take our time over the next 12 months to move in. For all our labors, we are rewarded with a magical view of the Ashokan Reservoir and the Hudson Valley.

When not working in New York and at our property, I enjoy cycling. I've done some licensed racing, but going out for long rides in the mountains is what I'm looking forward to getting back to.

I hope by exchanging these letters and pictures we can show you what our lives are like here. We feel very lucky to have our place here on the mountain, and I'm looking to the day when we will be able to share it with you. I know after reading your letters everything is going to be very special.

Paul Cohen

From: Ksweet 1072@aol.com
Sent: Tuesday, January 27, 1998 10:23PM
To: Jeanneb1@IBM.net
Subject: Lots of stuff

Hi, Thank you for my messages!

Kevin immediately alerted me that I had 3 messages, but he wouldn't read them until I got home. I think I will start by answering some of your questions from your letter that I just received.

I take two classes on Monday and Wednesdays. I expect to graduate in June. I work in downtown Cleveland for a large bank. A few months ago I was promoted to Key Accounts Manager, an Assistant Vice President level. I have been with the bank since July of 1990.

Regarding the family farm, it is still in the family per se, however my father is no longer involved. Currently he is an independent contractor and is busy all of the time. He recently had tendon transfer surgery and is recovering at home.

My mom works for the state and is also the organist at our church, and helps out her friend at a printing company when he needs an extra pair of hands. She also works on restoring antique trunks in the evenings and on weekends. They are both workaholics!

Growing up on the farm was fun. I played a lot with my cousins. Dad comes from a big family. We had dairy cows, rabbits, chickens, veal calves, and at times some pigs. It was a good experience. I love animals.

I have a question for you regarding your search for me. I would be interested in hearing more about the process that you had to go through, when you started, notifying New York State, and the response to the letters you mailed.

Paul, thank you for your message. I really enjoyed hearing your thoughts and learning a bit more about you. I would love to hear more about your work, it sounds really interesting. Thank your for supporting Jeanne in her search for me and continuing to support her as we venture ahead. She speaks fondly of you. I can hear it in her letters. Not everyone would/could be as understanding. That tells me a lot about you already. Well, I have to work on a school project. So good night for now.

Talk to you soon,
Karen

This was the first time that I asked about Jeanne's search. My curiosity was beginning to peak. I felt the pace was just right and I continued to delve into our backgrounds. The "getting-to- know- you" process was helping to bring me into adulthood for Jeanne, and a pretty comprehensive picture of her was emerging for me. Although my caution was still holding me back, I felt much more comfortable with our communications, which were reaching a more personal level. However, I still wasn't ready to suggest a meeting.

From: Jeanneb1@IBM.net
Date: Friday January 30, 1998 10:28 EST
To: Ksweet1072@aol.com
Subject: A Happy Ending

Hi, I missed talking to you yesterday.

Where do I begin? First of all, I stopped over at Dad's yesterday. I told him that you were asking about him. Anyway, he gave me an article that was front-page news in the local paper. It was about a 37 year old woman who had been reunited with her birth parents. There are some uncanny similarities, so I made a copy and hope to get that off tomorrow. I think that reading their story in some ways will help you understand things better.

So let me begin by telling you that I made a decision early on not to search for you until you were at least 19 to 21 years old. I did not want to confuse you in any way or upset your parents and ruin our chances of ever having a good relationship with each other. I had to repress my feelings for a long time. When the time was right, I was very fearful of rejection. I was afraid you would be angry and would not understand. So it took me awhile to get over this fear and move ahead. I was still living in California at the time and was not happy with my situation.

I suddenly began to feel an incredible desire to move back home and reconnect with my family. So in December, 1990, I moved home to start school in New Paltz. Anyway, to make a long story short, after talking with my sister I realized that I needed to find you. She had heard about an organization called ALMA (Adoptee's Liberty Movement Assoc.) and encouraged me to join. So that helped to get me to make up my mind to begin an active search. I wrote to the County Dept. of Social Services, I contacted a local attorney, and I searched the local college library for birth announcements. I also spent some time at the County Court house.

In 1992, I signed up with another registry called Soundex Registry, as well as joined a local support group for adoptees and birth parents. I met one woman who had found her mother. She really helped inspire and support me. She gave me the name of an organization called "Seekers of the Lost" and also put my name on the Internet with a registry. I contacted Seekers and they ran a computer search for all females born on 6/23/67 registered to vote in New York. I received a list of 250+ names. This is how the letter writing campaign got under way.

I continued to get leads from various sources on how to search for missing people and was finally referred by a former police officer/private investigator to a woman in

Texas, from the Rights of the Adoption and Information Bureau. She was a paralegal who had been successful in filing petitions to the court to open adoption records. She felt I had a good case, given the history of cancer in the family.

After the petition was filed, the judge agreed to proceed with the release of the information to another private investigator, Pat Rutherford of World Wide Tracers Inc. He was able to locate you within 24 hours after getting your name. However, he was unable to talk to you because your phone number was unlisted. I was in shock! Then within about 48 hours he spoke to you, and of course the rest is history.

It took a long time, but it sure was worth it!! I have this beautiful gift, this daughter that I am having a great time getting to know. What a happy ending and new beginning.

I am enclosing the article along with the medical history and a copy of your hospital records

Hope to hear from you soon.

Love, Jeanne

It was interesting to know that Jeanne's father had taken the trouble to cut out an article about an adoption search. What Jeanne did not know was that my mother had cut out the same article and sent it to me. I was still harboring a resentment toward Jeanne's father. After all, he had other grandchildren and I'm sure he loved them. I knew it was probably unjustified, but I could not help feeling like an abandoned grandchild. This seemed to be the only resentment left in me. I knew I had to get by it.

From: Ksweet1072@aol.com
Date: Saturday, January 31, 1998, 10:07 EST
To: Jeanneb1@IBM.net
Subject: A Happy Ending

Hi Jeanne,

Good Morning!

I spoke with my parents yesterday. You both must be on the same wavelength because she too sent the article from the local paper about the 37 year old woman's adoption story. I cried when I read it. It was very heartwarming.

She also sent me a poem I gave to my grandmother a long time ago. She was going through some papers and found it, so I wanted to share it with you so you can understand how much I loved my grandmother (my mom's mother)

When things are confused, I discuss them with you until they make sense.
When something good happens you are the first person I tell so I can share my happiness.
When I don't know what to do in a situation, I ask your opinion and weigh it heavily with mine.
When I am lonely, I call you because I never feel alone with you.
When I have a problem I ask for your help because your wise ness helps me solve it.
When I want to have fun, I want to be with you because you understand me.
When I want the truth about something, I call you because you are honest.

It is so essential to have you in my life. Thank you for being my friend and grandmother.

Author Unknown

I wish that I had dated this, but I know I was in high school. She was a great lady and I miss her terribly. Anyway, I wanted to re-read your e-mail on "the Search". I'm sure I'll have more questions for you.

I hope you have fun in the city this weekend. Do you have friends in the city as well? How far is your apartment from Central Park? How long does the train take? I took the train from Cleveland to Albany once and it wasn't bad, but both ways had delays.

I'll send you another message later. I just hoped you might get this before you leave for the weekend. I'll talk to you soon.
Karen

KAREN

I began to notice how the family members from both sides were as anxious as I was and ready to help in any way they could. I thought it was quite a coincidence that Jeanne's father and my mother had seen and cut out the same article. As I would later learn, this would be only one of the coincidences that would spring from this story. More bizarre coincidences were about to happen.

Newspaper article sent to me by my Mother and given to Jeanne by her Father.

KATEBOARDER SLAPPED

DOLAN ANSWERS
Independent editorial
18

HUDSON
21

The Independen

Found!

Excerpts from my birth records.

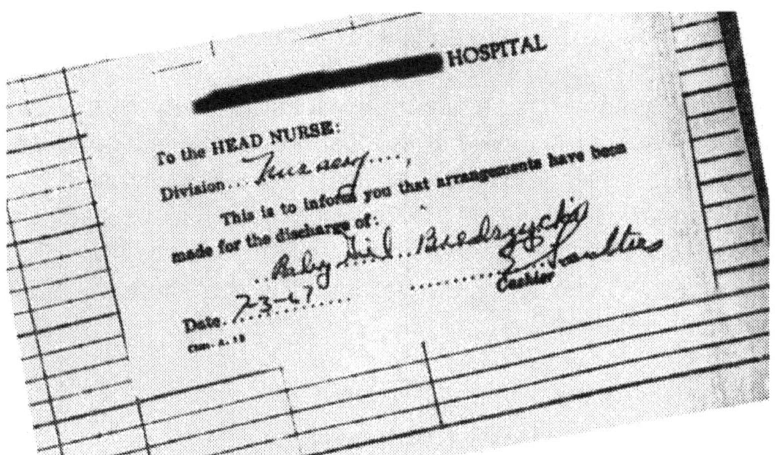

HOSPITAL

To the HEAD NURSE:

Division... Nursery...,

This is to inform you that arrangements have been made for the discharge of:

..Baby Girl..Biedrzycki

.... Cashier

Date. 7-3-67

BABY Girl Biedrzycki

DISCHARGED IN

CUSTODY OF

AT 7-3-67 (Date & Time)

SIGNED (Recipient)

WITNESS

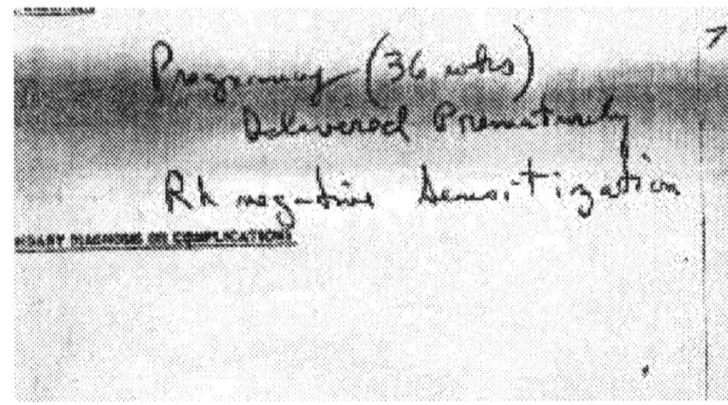

Pregnancy (36 wks)

Delivered Prematurely

Rh negative sensitization

...DARY DIAGNOSIS OR COMPLICATIONS

Jeanne's e-mail had stimulated much thought on my part. I realized how happy a life I was leading, just going on my way. I had a great job, a wonderful husband, a great family. I loved my work and we had an active social life. Until now, I had no problem with my identity. How things had changed! I was now forced to think about Jeanne and her years of searching. Her search effort affirmed the fact that I had been wanted; I wasn't just a mistake who had been easily discarded so as not to disgrace the family. I was beginning to come to grips with my feelings, and I began thinking more about Jeanne than myself.

From: Ksweet1072@aol.com
Date: February 2, 1998 18:42 EST
To: Jeanneb1@IBN.net
Subject: Just Some Thoughts

Hi, Jeanne

I keep re-reading "A Happy Ending" because it just tells me so much about what you actually went through to find me. I can't seem to find the right words to express how that makes me feel.

I can't imagine what it would be like to have to repress your feelings for so long. That must have been incredibly difficult. I can understand the feelings of rejection. I think that it could work both ways. When a child searches for his/her birth parent(s), he/she too risks that very same emotion. I guess for me, after you found me, I didn't have to worry about that because I knew you wanted to find me. However, I guess that I thought: Would you be proud of how I turned out? How I was raised?

Can you share with me what you and your sister talked about that convinced you to search? I would be really interested. You mentioned that when in CA, you had an incredible urge to move home and reconnect with your family. Kevin and I both feel that way also. We have been here three years and the move to Cleveland was a good experience for both of us, but we miss our families a great deal. However, we both need to finish school and would need to find good jobs back east before we could make such a big move again. But we miss the strength and love that family can provide when we are together. It is also important for our future children to be surrounded by all of their grandparents.

What year did you actually join ALMA? You also mentioned that you tried to look up birth announcements in the paper under my original name. I can also see by the hospital records that my original name was Michelle. How did you choose the name Michelle? I know it is probably weird for you to refer to me as Karen, after so many years of thinking of me as Michelle. You know I am not actually sure how my parents came up with my name, so I'll have to ask them. Anyway, Karen was quite a popular name in school. I graduated with six other Karens in my class.

The name Michelle is only something that my mother told me about recently so that I could have information to confirm with Pat Rutherford that what he was saying was true... and it was.

Can you also tell me more about your letter- writing campaign? I was so surprised that so many females were born in NYS on 6/23/67. How many responses did you get? Did you get telephone calls?
I will share with you my feelings the day that your form letter arrived. It was late April, on a Sunday and we had just gotten back from our Florida vacation, so of course the mail was piled up. In the pile was a letter from my mother. I opened it up and inside the letter was your letter addressed to my maiden name at my parent's address. At first I thought that Jeanne could be a friend from college and I didn't know her married name since I knew no other Jeannes. Now I am being honest, so I hope this does not hurt. As I read the letter, I felt this incredible shock come over me. I felt like I was two years old again and needed the things that were most comforting to me, my parents.

I called them immediately and my dad answered the phone. He could hardly understand me, I was crying so much. I said, "Get Mom on the phone". I wanted both of them to be on the phone. I could barely get the words out. I think I knew that minute that I was the person in that letter that for whom you were so desperately searching.

My mother felt so responsible for the shock I was feeling because she had forwarded me the letter. She wanted to get on the next train to be with me, but I had work commitments that would not permit me to take any time off to spend with her. I told her to wait and to come on Memorial Day weekend, and she and my father did.

You have to understand that it was just too much for me to digest. So I put your letter away for awhile. Periodically I would pull it out and re-read it. I talked to a few people, many of whom told me that it was my decision and I was in control as to what to do next. I needed time, so over the summer is when I read quite a few books that helped me gain a better understanding of how things were different in the Sixties.

During this period I had more questions in my head than ever before. I guess I was at peace with myself for so many years, that this was "all meant to be," there was a reason, and I didn't question it. I had a very loving family and great life of my own.

Kevin had not told me about our neighbor coming to the door with the message that a private investigator was looking for me. Kevin knew I was having a hard time with what to do, and he didn't want me to be upset if it was nothing. So the next day is when Kevin called Pat Rutherford, but Pat said he had to speak with me.

He mentioned to Kevin that he had been petitioned by the New York State Court due to medical reasons to get in touch with me. That's when Kevin called me at work. I was so upset I had to leave work. I remember crying the whole way home. It took me awhile to work up my nerve to call, as I wasn't sure about any of this.

Pat was a man who was sensitive, and he made it easy for me to talk to him. He welcomed my call. He told me the medical information and told me how wonderful you were. He said, "She cries for you every day". He told me that you never remarried because you wanted to keep your maiden name in case I was looking for you. He also told me that you had no other children. This news made me sad. Pat asked me if you could call, but I said it was too much for me. I told him that it would be okay for you to write.

He only had one request of me that day. He said he hoped that one day we would send him a picture of us together so that he could see us reunited.

So this is my side of the story. It was hard for me because all I could think about was how happy you must have been over your finding me. On the other hand, I was very confused about this news. After all, this was the first news about my birth mother in 30 years.

My parents and Kevin have been very supportive. Yet Kevin gets very anxious about us meeting. I have been thinking about it and spoke to my parents today. I still need to do some more thinking on this subject, but will let you know my thoughts soon.

Well, I must really go and do some work. Kevin is making dinner. Believe it or not, I do cook, it just seems that whenever I am talking to you he is in the kitchen!

Hope you had fun in the city. I look forward to hearing from you later in the week, because I will be in New Jersey on Tuesday and fly back to Cleveland on Wednesday, but go right to school.

Anxious to hear from you, Karen

KAREN

My husband Kevin had been following these events very carefully. He felt he wanted to write to Jeanne and Paul (as Paul had written to us) in order to keep himself involved in the developments. I could tell that this was one of the ways in which he was trying to support me. I welcomed his involvement. As much support as I was getting from my parents, I knew that I would probably fall apart if Kevin were not standing there with me.

From: Ksweet1072@aol.com
Sent: Tuesday, February 03, 1998 10:34 PM
To: Jeanneb1@IBN.net
Subject: My Life Story

Where do I begin? I was born in Niskayuna, New York and lived there all my life. I lived in the same house until I moved in with Karen in 1993. One of the hardest times in my life was when my parents got divorced. I was in fifth grade at the time. For the remainder of my life, I lived with my mother.

I think it was very beneficial to me growing up with my mother. I am very domestic, and probably contribute a lot more to Karen's and my relationship because of it. I was very fortunate to have had a mother who sacrificed so much for me. Times were tough, but we made it.

There is a silver lining to every story. Both of my parents remarried. I think they both found more suitable mates.

I couldn't have asked for a better situation. Everyone gets along. Whenever there are major functions like birthdays, holidays, or special events, everyone gets together and socializes like any other family. I was blessed with a sister from my father's second marriage. One bad part of living in Cleveland, so far away from home, is that I really miss seeing her grow up. I always wanted to have a brother or sister, and now that I do, I can't even watch her grow up.

After graduating from high school, I attended a local Community College. I majored in business administration. After I completed my studies, I continued my college education at a four year college in Albany, New York. I graduated in 1991 with a bachelor's degree in accounting. I was working with a wholesale music company while I was attending college. After graduation I was promoted to assistant controller. I worked there for about 9 months. I then took a position with waste management company in Albany as a district accountant. I was working there when I met Karen. We got married in September of 1994.

When we found out that we were going to relocate to Cleveland, I was able to transfer out to the Cleveland district with my company in the same role. After moving to Cleveland, I continued to work for the same company for approximately one year, and then took a position with a Title Insurance Company as the northern Ohio accounting manager. I was there for a little over one year. With no opportunities for advancement, I went to s local Bank as a financial analyst in the Corporate Accounting Department. I was not satisfied with the position, and left after three months. I am now working for an International company as a recruiting manager for accounting and financial professionals. I love my job and the people I work with.

I am presently attending a College in Cleveland and am working for my MBA. I am over halfway finished, and will graduate in December of this year. In my spare time, I enjoy tennis, golf, music, and jet skiing. Karen and I used to be big skiers before we moved to "flat" Cleveland. We really miss home and the beautiful surroundings of the New England area.

I am glad that you ended up finding Karen. At times I think I am just as excited, if not more so, when we receive your letters and now e-mail. I look forward to continuing our relationship and meeting both of you in the future. Thank you for being so understanding and patient with Karen and the whole situation. I support her 100 percent and I believe that this is beneficial to everyone. Have a great day, and we will both look forward to your next message.

Kevin

From: Jeanneb1@IBM.net
Date: February 5, 1998, 12:36am EST
To: Ksweet1072@aol.com
Subject: Letter in process

Dear Karen,

I received your letter along with the one from Kevin. They were both very meaningful and important to me in many ways. It was a lot of stuff I needed to hear. I have been working on a letter to answer all of your questions and to share more feelings about a lot the things that you talked about. Once again, I want to take my time with all of this because it is a bit more difficult to put into words...

Did you get the medical history and medial records that I sent? Let me know if you have questions about that...

I love you both, thanks so much! Goodnight!

Jeanne

From: Jeanneb1@IBM.net
Date: February 6, 1998, 19:32:04 EST
To: Ksweet1072@aol.com
Subject: Finally finished

Dear Karen:

I just got back from New York City. The city is nice for a few days but I'm always glad to get home, I guess I am just a country girl at heart. I was also anxious to check my mail because I was missing you! So of course I was very excited to have two letters. It was so nice to hear from Kevin. I really enjoyed reading his life story. It told me a lot about his character and what is important in his life. He sounds very caring and sensitive. I really appreciate his enthusiastic support…it means a lot to me.

I have to tell you that your story really touched my heart, and of course the tears started to flow. Yes, it was extremely difficult for me all of those years. Deep down I was definitely not happy… the memory was always there. A piece of me was missing. The way that I tried to explain it to Paul was that it was like having a family member who was "missing in action." I knew that you were out there somewhere, but I didn't know where, didn't know if you were happy and healthy or even if you were still alive. I thought about you so many times and tried to picture your face. I guess when I moved away from home I was running away from the pain. So when I moved back home, it all came back to me and I was feeling quite depressed.

I tried not to get my hopes up too high during the search, but it was hard. The search did help to give me hope. Paul kept telling me not to worry because it would happen. When we started the new house, I remember telling Paul, "Now I have everything that I want, my new house and you, but there is still one thing that was still missing: my daughter." He told me he just knew that one day you would come to visit! That really helped to keep my hopes alive.

You asked me how I decided upon the name Michelle. To be honest with you, I don't exactly know how that came about. I do know that I have always liked that name. Did you know your middle name was Jeanne? This just made me think of a question for you. Did your parents receive any non-identifying information about me? What were you told, if anything? Did you know of the circumstances?

Finally, I want to tell you that you definitely touched my heart when you told me that one of your first thoughts when I found you was, "Would I be proud of you?" And the way you were raised?" What that said to me was that my opinion matters to you, and that made me feel pretty special. So I want to tell you that I am extremely proud of you and the way that you were raised. So far I see a very beautiful, loving, sensitive, well-educated, hard-working young woman. You have goals and a direction in life. You have a beautiful home and a great job. You have found a wonderful man to share your life with, and look forward to having a family. I don't think that any mother could possibly ask for anything more. Finding you was a wonderful thing, but to find you so happy and secure was an added bonus.

Your parents deserve a lot of credit. Obviously they are very loving people with good moral values. They are honest and hard-working and provided you with a happy and secure family life. This is everything that I could have ever hoped for you. My last words to the social worker when I had to sign the papers, were "Make sure you find her a good home." I think that God must have been listening! Yes, I am very proud of who you are and who you have become. I am very proud that you are my daughter.

I have to tell you that I was thrilled when you said that you and Kevin are hoping to move back to the area. That was something that I was going to ask you about. It would definitely be another dream come true for me. What a wonderful thing it would be to say, "I'm going to visit my daughter today to have lunch!" Anyway the thought of you being so close is very exciting for me. I'll start praying for good jobs here for you and Kevin.

So I guess that I'm finally finished. I want to get this off to you. I will check my e-mail periodically throughout the evening just in case.

Lots of Love,
Jeanne

I was very happy that Jeanne was proud of me and my parents. It obviously meant a great deal to her. Due to my family upbringing and the high regard in which I hold my parents, I am certainly the type that wants my parents to be proud of me. Subconsciously, I wanted my birth mother to proud of me too. I didn't want her to be disappointed with what she had found. I also wanted her to know she had made the right decision to give me to two wonderful people, my mom and dad.

From: Ksweet1072@aol.com
Date: February 7, 1998, 9:45 EST
To: Jeanneb1@IBM.net
Subject: Off to School

Hi Jeanne,

Thank you for your heart-warming letter. It was very emotional for me to read. I have lots of things that I want to share with you. However, for the moment it will have to wait. I need to go to meet a friend at school to work on a project. I will write back this afternoon.

I'm trying to jot down all of the things I want to say later, so I don't forget.

Have a great day!
Karen

This may have sounded abrupt, but all this was coming at a very hectic time in my life. I was busy with my job and my night school studies. I worked all day, went to night school, and still had to maintain my home. Most of my spare time was being taken up by my studies and preparation for my classes and exams. There were also papers to write. I had to learn to keep some of these emotional things on hold, or it would have distracted me from my work. I could only hope that Jeanne would understand.

From: Ksweet1072@aol.com
Date: Saturday, February 7, 1998 3:52pm EST
To : Jeanneb1@ibm.net
Subject: My response to "Finally Finished"

Hi Jeanne,

I was anxious to hear back from you, so I checked my e-mail several times yesterday before Kevin and I went on our 'DATE'.

Kevin called me during the day to tell me that he had made a reservation at the Ritz Carlton for dinner at 7:30 p.m. He was going out for a drink with his boss and would be home to pick me up at 7:00. Well, of course, I had to get a new dress. I had my eye on this long black dress, so I wanted to surprise Kevin and I zipped to the mall and it was still there.

So I quickly got ready before he got home because I didn't want him to see me in my dress until we got to the Ritz. Anyway, I surprised him. It felt nice to be on a date again. It is very easy to get lost in the routine of the week.

When I arrived home I wanted to see if you had sent your letter, and you had. Kevin and I both read it together and the tears just rolled down my face. Kevin was very comforting, he wiped the tears away as we read on together.

Kevin thinks the more we write the more he notices how much alike we are. He sees the emotions jump off the page. I know what he means, I see it too.

Anyway, your letter was beautiful and very touching, yet I can see the pain in your words when you talk about certain parts of your life, and about the guilt and great void you felt. I keep turning this over in my mind. I think that sometimes God tests our faith. For me, this is how I look at this new piece of my life... to now look back 30 years and have answers and find the truth.

After hearing from you initially, I would tell myself that I need to look to God. After all, I didn't have a fatal disease, there was no death in the family, etc. So, even though this was incredibly shocking at first, I have found an incredible peace as well.

Thank you for the medical information. Reading the hospital records was very weird for me. To see "baby girl", to know that was me, and to see your name as my mother was very surreal. I never knew I was born 4 weeks early. Did the doctor say why I came so early? I know 1 month is not abnormal.

Could you share with me some thoughts about being pregnant with me? I guess *one thing I have always thought about* is that I will never have a picture of my mother pregnant with me. (Of course, I know that you probably had some very mixed emotions during this time, so I will understand if it is difficult for you to respond.)

Were you able to stay at home during your pregnancy? I have read that a lot of girls had to go to homes. I know I am asking you to go back to a difficult time in your life, but I guess I need to know your feelings about me, this life that was growing inside you. I think often about being a mother and wanting to really enjoy this beautiful experience. I believe that children are gifts from God.

I have really enjoyed getting to know you and building the beginning of our relationship. However, you are only half of who I am. Hopefully, in time, maybe you could tell me more about my birth father... I haven't really been focusing on that topic as much because I have had so many questions for you. But please understand that it would not be fair to me to only know half of who I am. I decided to have a relationship with you, and what comes with that is to know the whole story. I would never want to purposely upset you with these questions or bring up mixed emotions, but it would only be "half the book" without these answers.

Thank you so much for being honest. I feel like I can ask you anything and you will answer. I feel as though we are developing a friendship. Each day I feel more and more comfortable with our relationship. I feel the love you have for me, and it is more genuine than I could have ever imagined. Thank you for that unconditional love, it makes me feel warm inside. It is amazing to think that a person I have never met could love me so much...

You are in my thoughts often lately.

Karen

P.S. My parents were not told anything about you when I was given to them. They didn't even know my name was Michelle until a year later when they had to go to court to finalize the adoption. Actually, my mom and dad are visiting for a week, they are coming out on the 13th. She said she would send you a message.

They have been great through this. I know when the time comes and we decide to meet, they too would like to meet you.

Karen

I felt that Jeanne was being very honest with all her answers and in sharing her feelings. I was sure she would be all right with answering some of these hard questions. I felt we had established enough trust, judging by her willingness to share her innermost thoughts and emotions. It was obviously time to take the next step. We couldn't hide anything from each other, no matter how difficult the circumstances. This was also the first time I had made any mention about our meeting each other in person.

From: Jeanneb1@IBM.net
Date: February 8, 1998 9:50:24 EST
To : Ksweet1072@aol.com
Subject: Good Things

Good morning! I received your beautiful letter. I have re-read it many times. It is true that all of this is a bit difficult, but I'm really okay with it. The more we talk, the better I feel. I think that is very healing for me, so don't worry. I'm glad that you feel like you can tell me anything, because that is exactly what I want. I also don't have any problem telling you whatever you want to know about your birth father. In fact, I was actually waiting for you to ask.

I wasn't sure how you felt about that since I know how important all of this is to you. So let me gather my thoughts a little more and then I will get a letter off to you. I promise.

XX,
Jeanne

JEANNE:

It was difficult to think about the circumstances of my getting pregnant. However, the relief of knowing that Karen felt she could ask me anything far outweighed any hurt I still harbored on this subject. I thought back to my plan to get married, and to my parents finding out about my boyfriend's other girlfriend. I remember him coming to our house and my parents ordering him not to see me again. With those images racing around in my head, I began thinking about the next letter to her, although I received two more e-mails from her before I was able to get it written.

From: Ksweet1072@aol.com
Date: Saturday, February 8, 1998 12:44pm EST
To: Jeanneb1@IBM.net
Subject: Chat online

Hi, Did you know we could actually chat online (I don't mean in a chat room.) But if we are both online at the same time I can send you an instant message and you can respond.

Let me know if you would like to try this. We could pick a time maybe later or on Tuesday night.

I received your "good things", I was glad to hear your response. I was a little worried that I asked some very tough questions that might stir up a lot of buried emotions. So, I was relieved to hear that you are really okay with all of this.

Here is another quick thought I had on how this all helps me too! Before you found me, sometimes I would have thoughts of being a "mistake" or "being unwanted." I could not understand why things had happened the way they did. It was very difficult to explain these feelings to Kevin. He would also try to encourage me and reassure me that God brought me into this world and that God does not make mistakes. I didn't let these thoughts overly consume me because I was mostly at peace with it and very happy! I'm a very grounded person and often count my blessings. Yet it is natural to get the blues sometimes, and this is when it would really bother me.

So overall, this is very healing for me as well, and to know I'll never really have those unwanted feelings again, because I'll know the whole story! Most importantly, this has been extremely positive so far and I am feeling really good!! I'll be anxious to get the letter that you are working on. I know it will take some time to compose.

Talk to you soon,
Karen

I was ready to learn more about the other genetic side of me. I prepared myself for what I was about to learn. Many questions kept popping up in my head. Did my birth father want me as much as my birth mother? Did circumstances also prevent him from keeping me? Or did he simply not want any part of me? I was prepared to learn the truth and live with it.

I never really shared these thoughts with anyone, except Kevin. I tried to explain how hurtful it was to feel that my mother did not want me. I knew I was expressing a childlike emotional fear, but it is a kind of feeling that never really goes away. I thought a natural child could never understand this concept.

From: Ksweet@aol.com
Date: Saturday, February 8, 1998 6:40pm
To: Jeanneb1@IBM.net
Subject: How to chat together

Hi, guess what. Kevin just told me that you have to have America Online in order for us to chat. We chat with his parents "live." Come to think of it, they have AOL as well.

Oh well, it was a good thought anyway.

Today I called my mother because I was a little worried about her. I was very concerned about her feelings. I have been sharing our conversations with my parents so they won't feel closed out. Mom said it was a little hard, but also believes it is good for both of us. I told her I am a little bit of each of you (her, Dad, and you). I think she too has seen a lot of you in me, just by what I have been telling her and that is why I know it could make her feel somewhat insecure. I am trying to reassure her and keep her included. I hope you don't mind.

I will talk to you soon.
Goodnight!
Karen

I learned later that all this had been very overwhelming for my mother. She was putting up a good front for my sake, but on the inside she was feeling vulnerable and threatened. I think she was beginning to see some of the similarities Jeanne and I shared in our genetic link, and Mom was suddenly beginning to question the strength of our own mother-daughter relationship.

This was, of course, understandable, but completely unjustified. My parents always believed in me. Mom brought me up to be independent and self-reliant. They worked hard and sacrificed all their lives to give their children everything possible in life. It was because of them that I grew into someone with a plan, aware of the direction in which I wanted to go. They were good about letting go when we moved to Cleveland even though they would have liked us to stay in the area. I had to make sure that Mom and Dad would always know that no one could ever take their place.

From: Jeanneb1@IBM.net
Date: Monday, February 9, 1998 6:04pm EST
To: Ksweet1072@aol.com
Subject: Some answers

Hi, I wanted to tell you that your date with Kevin sounded very romantic. I love all that kind of stuff too! Paul is very sweet but he needs a little help in this department, although he is getting better. I just got your most recent message about chatting online. My friend Linda from work had mentioned something about it, so I was aware that it was possible. I think that it would be great. You'll have to let me know how it works. We are going out to dinner with our contractor and his wife this evening. If it is not too late we can try tonight or else I will be home Tuesday night.

You said that it was really weird to read your hospital records. I'm not surprised. I kind of imagined that it would be fairly intense, but knew that it would be an important part of the puzzle. In a way I think it sort of validates who you are and where you came from. It's something tangible and I think that is very important. I feel that it is the most natural thing in the world to want to know the details of your birth, your "roots" and where you came from. You also said that your parents were not given any information. I'm assuming that they did not know the name of the hospital. Is that correct? Anyway, you also asked if the doctor knew why you came early. I was never told anything. I guess there is a possibility that the due date was miscalculated. Also being a teen mother may have had something to do with it.

There is an important thing that I want to stress to you before I continue any further. Yes, it is true that my pregnancy was not planned and I was very frightened and confused when it happened. This does not mean that you were unwanted. I was 15 years old and I started seeing this boy who was 20. I really thought that I was in love. Of course, at 16 you don't really understand the meaning of love. But at least at the time, in my heart I would say that you were conceived in love. I didn't tell you this before, but the original plan was for us to get married. After I found out that I was pregnant, I heard that he had been seeing another girl. My parents did not really approve of him, so when they heard this they cancelled the marriage plans. They proceeded to make arrangements for me to go to a home in Westchester County. I can remember driving down there to visit. I did not like the idea at all. I guess that I was scheduled to go about a week or so before you were actually born. Because I went into labor prematurely, they decided to just take me to the local hospital.

You said you were curious to know how I felt when I was pregnant with you. I guess, as I look back on it now, I can remember an incredible sense of wonder and awe the first time I could feel movement. That was very special and I have never forgotten that. I also felt incredible sense of peace when I felt you move. I knew that you were there, and you were comforting to me. Even though there was a lot of confusion during this time, there are moments that I can look back on and treasure. It really is a beautiful experience. As painful as all this has been, I can honestly say that I am thankful that I was able to have the experience in my lifetime.

I also agree with you 100% that children are a gift from God, because to me this was a miracle. From the moment I could feel you move and was able to feel this new life inside me, a bond was formed that can never be broken.

We have to leave shortly for dinner. We are going to one of our favorite restaurants in Woodstock. It has a very romantic setting next to a stream that is lit up at night.

Talk to you later,
XX
Jeanne

KAREN

Jeannie was right about the hospital records. The experience of reading them was very intense. Seeing the term "baby girl Biedrzycki" and to know that it was me is very difficult to describe. It represented the facts of my birth and my connection to my birth mother. Yet it was difficult for me to digest. Never having known anything about my birth, it still did not seem real to me.

From: Jeanneb1@IBM.net
Date: Monday, February 9, 1998, 12:39pm EST
To: Ksweet1072@aol.com
Subject: More Good Stuff

Hi, I really hope your mom is doing okay. I know that all of this hasn't been easy for any of us. I think that I can understand how she must feel. I'm glad she thinks that this is a good thing. Please reassure her that all I want is for you to be happy and for everyone to feel comfortable. So I feel good about you sharing our conversations with your parents. I also want them to know that I would be very happy to meet both of them.

It fills my heart with joy to know that you think all of this has really been a positive thing for you and you are feeling really happy about things. It is so nice that there are no more secrets now...and that there is only truth and love. That feels pretty good to me too!

I have to get ready to go to work soon, so I promise that I will write tomorrow and tell you more about your birth father. I'm sure that I will also have lots of other thoughts to share with you by then. Oh, one question, what are your parent's first names?

Talk to you soon. XO, Jeanne

From: Jeanneb1@IBM.net
Date: Monday, February 9, 1998, 9:35pm EST
To: Ksweet1072@aol.com
Subject: Just Thinking

Hi, I know that you have school tonight so you will get back late. I hope that you are keeping up with your work OK with all of these distractions. This morning when I was lying in bed I was thinking about what I wrote last night. I said that there was truth and love, but I forgot to add peace. You said that you have found a greater sense of peace because now you will never feel unwanted again.

For me, the guilt was the hardest thing. Many of the things you have been saying in your most recent letters have helped to replace my guilt feelings with an incredible sense of peace of mind and happiness that I haven't felt in 30 years. I also think that for me, the final stage of "closure" will come when I see you in person. I need to touch you and hold you and then everything will be OK. I am a very affectionate person. I like to give lots of hugs. I hope you won't mind.

Much love,
Jeanne

P.S. I've been meaning to tell you about my name. It's pronounced "Jeann-ee" (Jeanie) even though I don't use the i. All of my family and close friend call me "Jeannie," although I spell it Jeanne, and for business purposes I use Jean.

From: Ksweet1072@aol.com
Date: Tuesday, February 10, 1998 7:31pm
To: Jeanneb1@IBM.net
Subject: Some questions to "Some Answers"

The past few days have been so busy. I am trying to catch my breath. I have been spending a lot of time at school. Work has been equally as demanding. I really can't wait for this school thing to be over.

Anyway, thank you for sharing the information about my birth father. Could you tell me a little more? Does he know about me? Have you ever spoken with him again? Do you know where he is now? I think I just have a desire to know some answers, not to look for him or anything like that. My zodiac sign is Cancer, and I am very cautious.

Thank you for reassuring me that I wasn't unwanted. I do believe that if things could have worked out or if you had had more control over the situation, I would have been very wanted in your life. Your commitment to me now is a sure sign of that.

More and more I have thoughts of starting a family. My school is nearly finished and it is something Kevin and I are talking about more frequently. Actually, we agreed on this some time ago. We feel our education is very important in this competitive workplace and juggling a full time job, school, and a baby would be too much.

We also want to save as much as we can. I would really like to be able to stay home, at least for a few years if possible. We have no family to help us out here and I feel strongly that the family values which will make our children feel loved right from the start are very important.

Kevin just walked in the door and I have to get dinner ready, so I will close.

By the way, in your “just thinking” letter you mentioned that you are very affectionate. This is another trait we have in common.

Take care,
Karen
Say Hi to Paul

From: Jeanneb1@IBM.net
Date: Thursday, February 12,1998, 5:46pm EST
To: Ksweet1072@aol.com
Subject: The other half of the book

Karen,

Last night I jotted down a lot of my latest thoughts. First I want to tell you that your birth father's name is ****. He had dark hair, stood about 5'10" and was good looking. I saw him once after you were born. He knew I had given you up for adoption. He showed no interest, and I never saw or heard from him again.

I want you to know that I am feeling very excited and "upbeat" about everything. I think your decision to take things a bit slow was probably a very wise one. It has given us the time that we needed to "bridge the gap" and to reconnect and bond with each other. I also think a trust has been established between us, and so now we can be honest with our feelings...now we can be friends. As I have said before, I feel that God has given us this second chance together. So I am determined to make the most of it. I feel that if we can be friends and I can have a close relationship with you now, that would be my salvation. I can't think of anything else that is more important in my life. This is my #1 priority. I have already told you how happy I would be if you and Kevin moved back to New York. That would certainly give us the option of spending a lot more time together.

Hi to Kevin and I'll talk to you later.
XXOO Jeanne

From: Ksweet1072@aol.com
Date: Thursday, February 12, 1998 6:43pm
To: Jeanneb1@IBM.net
Subject: New Chapters in the Book

Hi! This sure has been a long week and I am feeling quite stretched at both ends. Work is very busy and school continues to be time-consuming. Anyway, my parents should be here when I get home from work tomorrow. I can't wait. My brother is coming too.

My brother David is older, 33, and he is also adopted. His situation is a little different. He is mentally handicapped. My parents got him when he was a few months old and already he had been placed in a few different foster homes. He is very introverted with his feelings. I love him, but it has been difficult for us to be close.

I can remember all the frustrations my parents had with things while growing up. Fighting with the schools, teaching him the little things that come easy for you and me, like counting change and telling time. They tried very hard to get him into a group environment with peers. Today he lives at home. He drives and is able to work. He is a very dependable and reliable worker. He needs structure and doesn't adapt to change very well. He likes to visit because he doesn't get very many opportunities to travel.

I guess I feel that was something I wanted to share with you. I think it tells you more about my parents and my family. My sister, Annie, is my parents natural child. They didn't think they could have children. My mom told me that when she and my dad had to go to court a year ago after I was adopted to finalize things, my mother was four months pregnant with my sister. The court asked my parents if they still wanted me because my sister would be their third child. She said, "Absolutely!" They still wanted me. It was at court that she first heard my given birth name was Michelle, but they had read it off so quickly in finalizing the procedures that that was all she knew.

Anyway, thank you for telling me more about my birth father. I guess my feelings are indifferent. What I mean is that after reading your news, I really don't feel any connection with this person. Perhaps in the future questions might arise, but for now I feel satisfied. It was weird to read that all of you lived close to the town where I grew up. Strange, I often had a feeling that you probably were never very far away from me.

How did you and Paul actually meet? It sounds like you have a lot in common. Pat Rutherford mentioned on the phone that you and he had been together for a long time and it would be a dream come true to have me at your wedding. Are there any plans?

Karen

From: Jeanneb1@IBM.net
Date: Thursday, February 12, 1998 10:20pm EST
To: Ksweet1072@aol.com
Subject: Response to "New Chapters of the book"

Hi, I enjoyed reading "new chapters of the book". It made me think a lot about what it must have been like growing up with your brother. I guess you must have had to help him a lot even though he was older. I'm sure that it probably made you a much more sensitive and caring person. I think that I might have told you that my experience with the man I take care of has changed my perspective on life. I am constantly reminded of all the things that I have that I should be thankful for. I also wanted to know more about your parent's decision to adopt. Because you had told me about your sister so I wasn't sure about all of that. I'm glad that you told me the story.

Speaking of stories, I will tell you the story of how I met Paul the next time I talk to you. I'm looking forward to many new happy chapters of the book of the future.

XXOO, Jeanne

From: Ksweet1072@aol.com
Date: Friday, February 13, 1998 7:58 pm
To: Jeanneb1@IBM.net
Subject: My parents are here

Hi, my parents arrived today at 4:00 p.m. They hit a little snow outside Buffalo. Your package also arrived today. Thank you for my Valentine gifts. You'll have to thank Paul's mother for my mittens, that was very thoughtful of her. Did you make the headband?

My mom wants to wish you and Paul a Happy Valentines Day.

I'll talk to you soon.
Karen

On this visit, Dad assumed the support role for both my mother and me. I don't think he felt as uneasy about the situation as Mom did, since the "father figure" was not being threatened. My father is a giant teddy bear, six feet four inches tall and weighing 285 pounds. He wears a size 14 shoe and his hands are as big as a baseball glove. At least they seemed that way when we were kids. All my boyfriends brought me home on time.

Dad loves his family very much and would do anything for his children. He is kind and gentle, albeit a bit of a mischief-maker. He enjoys just being near us, even when we are all doing different things. I think that makes him feel close to us.

From: Jeanneb1@IBM.net
Date: Saturday, February 14, 1998 02:29 EST
To: Ksweet1072@aol.com
Subject: From the heart

XOXOXOXOXOXOXOXOXOXOXOXOXOXOXOXOXO
XO
HAPPY VALENTINES DAY TO ALL!
WITH LOVE FROM THE HEART

PAUL & JEANNE
XOXOXOXOXOXOXOXOXOXOXOXOXOXOXOXOXO
XO

Hi, Karen and Kevin.

Your package arrived yesterday. I loved the cards, the wedding mementos, the beautiful little picture, and the warm thoughts that came with them!! Thank you for making me feel so special. Today I feel very thankful for all the love and support of family and friends during this special time in both our lives. Without them, it wouldn't have been so easy. So I agree that we are both very lucky to be loved so much. Valentine's Day is about "LOVE" and I think that is what all this is about.

A special hello and thank you to your mom & dad from Paul and me. Have a wonderful day. Talk to you later.
Much Love,
Jeanne & Paul

P.S. Paul is having trouble with skunks in our back yard. Any suggestions as to how we can get rid of them?

From: Ksweet1072@aol.com
Date: Saturday, February 14, 1998 10:10 am
To: Jeanneb1@IBM.net
Subject: Skunks on Valentine's Day

Regarding the skunks, my dad thinks that skunks don't like mothballs. So try to put some in the hole without catching the skunk in a defensive position. Attempt with caution.

My mom's advice: stay clear! They shouldn't be out this time of year. However, with El Niño it has been warmer, so this could be why they are out.

Hope you have a special day together. Kevin got me a really nice card.

Looking forward to talking with you later.
Karen

From: Ksweet1072@aol.com
Date: Saturday, February 21, 1998 9:25:19 EST
To: Jeanneb1@IBM.net
Subject: The house is quiet again

Good Morning,

The house is quiet again. My parents and brother left yesterday morning around 7:15 a.m. They were heading to the east side to see my aunt.

It was really nice having them here. My dad loves to do little things to help us around the house. If he doesn't visit the hardware store, he goes through withdrawal.

My mom spent some time reading through all of our e-mails to each other. I know that this has been a little more difficult for her than for my dad. I guess that is understandable. My dad told me that it's been very emotional for her. I have sensed this, and that is why I want to make sure that she feels included. By the end of the week she seemed to feel a lot better. Spending some "together" time was beneficial to her because I know she has been reassured.

My parents never thought they could have children. The doctors said the only way they could have children was to adopt. So they adopted my brother first. When they received the call for me, they hadn't anticipated that getting a second child would come so quickly. My mom had to call my cousin, who was expecting, and ask for her crib back. They hadn't even picked out names. She told me they chose my name from a baby book while on the way to pick me up. They both agreed on Karen Eileen.

Mom said they took me to her mother first to meet the family. They were all really nervous to pick me up because I was so small. Anyway, that is a little more information that my mom shared, but she said it all happened so quickly, this is all they really knew. The county had also told her that you were from another county. That is all they were told about you.

I hope to hear what you have been up to and your recent thoughts. I am in a really good mood this morning...

I'll talk to you later.
Karen

It was at this point that I decided it was time for me to write to Jeanne. I decided to use the old fashioned type mail with which I felt comfortable.

February 16, 1998

Dear Jeanne,
My husband told me when the time came for me to write to you, I would know. I believe it must be now.

I spent most of today reading your letters to Karen and looking over the medical records. I will never know how you felt some thirty years ago, just as I cannot tell you how I feel now, for I am so unable to put my feelings into words.

Harold (Karen's dad) and I have always considered Karen to be a gift from *God* and *You* and we only hope we can continue to share that gift which is so precious.

Karen is so loving, caring, considerate, understanding, and beautiful. But most of all, she is ours, "yours and mine." She is a wonderful blend of both of us, and you are to be as proud of her as her dad and I are.

May God bless and guide you into the future.

Karen's Mom,
Mary Lou

From: Jeanneb1@IBM.net
Date: Sunday, February 22, 1998 13:05:51 EST
To: Ksweet1072@aol.com
Subject: A new day

Dear Karen,

I remember you mentioning that your mom said she wanted to write me a letter. I guess I thought she meant an e-mail. Anyway, when you told me that she left I assumed she changed her mind. I went to the post office yesterday because I hadn't checked my mail the day before. I found a letter waiting for me from your mom. I could feel my heart pounding and I kind of took a deep breath. I sensed the emotions that I knew would be in this letter, and I needed to prepare myself. What I found inside was someone struggling with her own feelings but who had room in her heart to extend her hand to me. That tells me a lot about her. It was so beautifully written, very honest and sincere. I think reading all of our correspondence gave her a lot of insight into how difficult this has been for me.

She said, "I will never know how you felt some 30 years ago." I think that she must realize by now that this was the ultimate sacrifice for me. She went on to say that she and your dad always considered you to be a gift from both "God and me". Anyway, I think that after spending time with you, she felt secure enough to say that she just wants to continue to "share" my gift to them. She also reassured me that your are "ours" (hers and mine,) and how you are wonderful blend of both. She also said, "You must be as proud of her as her dad and I are".

This touched something very deep inside me. I re-read it many times and couldn't get over how beautiful these words were to me. I have a tremendous amount of respect for her because I know that none of this was easy for her to say. But I know she understands my feelings as a mother. I also think that she understands how important this is for you, and she loves you enough to open her heart to me. I know that in time we will become friends. After all, we have something pretty special to us in common.

Although all of this was very positive, it brought me back to the most difficult time in my life. Suddenly I saw a 16-year- old again who was feeling so alone with this tremendous sense of loss and despair. I missed you so much, it felt like a part of me had died. On the other hand, I could now picture your mom and dad driving together to pick you up and take you to her mom's house to meet the family. I could just imagine how happy and excited everyone was with this wonderful little "bundle of joy". So I kept thinking how my pain brought so much happiness to someone else. In some ways, that was very comforting to me, knowing something so good had come from all of this. But at the same time I began to mourn the loss of all of those wonderful moments. I realize that I can never change any of that and it hurts me so much. I have often thought to myself, just as you said, that you wonder " why did all of this happen to me?" I just couldn't make sense of it. This isn't the way it was supposed to be. A girl is supposed to get married and have children and live happily ever after. Well, I guess life doesn't always turn out the way you think it should.

Anyway, all of these thoughts were floating around in my head and I was having a difficult time. I spent most of the day outside helping Paul. I think that helped because if I sat down too long I would start to cry. But I think all of it was good for me. I needed to get it out so that I could try to resolve some of these things in my mind.

I talked to Paul about it a lot, he is so sweet and understanding. He just lets me talk and cry, and then we move on and keep working. At the end of the day we stood around and watched the bonfire burn down. I threw a final branch on the fire and in my mind it symbolized the pain and guilt of the past. I know that I have to go backwards for awhile so I can put some of these things to rest. Then I can move ahead. So I feel much better today, now that my thoughts are becoming clearer. It's a new day and I know things will be okay. I love you so much, and I just want everything to be nice for all of us. I hope that one day we can all feel like a family.

I need to start to get ready to leave by two o'clock. I won't be back until Thursday morning and I'll check my mail before I go. I will work on a letter to your mom while I'm gone. I look forward to talking to you when I get home.

Much love,
Jeanne

It was about that time that I received the following letter from Karen's sister, Annie. I can't describe how good it made me feel at the time. It meant a lot to me.

Jeanne,

I hope you don't think this too bold of me, but I felt I had to say a few things. I'm not one for holding my tongue.

I really would like to thank you. I know that having to give up a child is probably the hardest thing anyone can do. From what I know, I can understand your situation. I wanted to thank you for giving her up. She and I are not much alike, but I love her and God made sure she had a pretty good childhood with a family that loves her very much.

I don't always understand her and she very seldom understands me. However, as we have gotten older we have started to build a relationship that anyone would be happy to have. I just wanted to say thank you. God made a child, he sent her to us through you. You should be very proud of yourself.

Annie

From: Ksweet1072@aol.com
Date: February 23, 1998 9:04 p.m.
To: Jeanneb1@IBM.net
Subject: Response to a New Day

Dear Jeanne:
I knew my mom was going to send you a letter, but I didn't know what she was going to write. I think she needed to collect her thoughts. She had spent a lot of time reading our letters so that she could begin to understand your situation, the pain, guilt, and loss you felt. She found that you were not someone to feel threatened by, but a woman struggling with herself, and trying to make sense of the past and what was happening now.

I knew it would probably be difficult for you to hear from my mother. I think that is natural. I'm sure many thoughts did rush through your head as you pondered opening the card. Maybe she was going to tell you to leave "her" daughter alone and that you had chosen to give me up. Maybe she would tell you that you had no right to get to know me, that she was the mother that had raised me.

But my mother is not this kind of woman. Of course she was very threatened at first, but my mom is a very warm and open-minded and open- hearted person. She has always encouraged me to do things, believe in myself, and even after reading our letters she encouraged me to give "us" a chance. I attribute a lot of my success to my mother for letting me spread my wings and telling me to take chances.

I was a little worried because I hadn't heard from you and hoped that things were okay. My thoughts are that I see a bright future ahead for us and feel optimistic about how things have progressed. We just need time to continue to build our relationship and to get to know each other.

I think the hardest questions for everyone thus far have been answered and we are at a good pace. Let's continue to share our thoughts and our feelings, I think it helps us to better understand each other.

Take care, Karen

From: Jeanneb1@IBM.net
Date: February 26, 1998, 18:14:40 EST
To: Ksweet1072@aol.com
Subject: Just what I needed

My dear Karen,

I was only gone for three days, but it seemed like forever because I missed you and wanted to talk to you. I couldn't wait to get home this morning to check my mail and sure enough, I found your e-mail along with a picture.

Your letter "A new day" was very sweet. It absolutely warmed my heart. Of course I cried, but they were tears of joy. Thank you so much for reassuring me about everything. Just to hear you say all of those things really helps. I am so happy to know that you see a bright future ahead for us. I know that there are many "special moments" yet to come and it is important to focus on that now. I'm sorry if I worried you. I kind of hated to leave because I was afraid of that. But Paul said its okay... that it was important for you to know when I was having a hard time. I think he was right, because writing it all down has helped a lot. That just made me think ... when I look back on the time Paul and I have been together I realize some of the hardest times have brought us closer together. Like when my mom and his dad died. Or when my dad had cancer surgery or when his mom was in the hospital. There is nothing more important than love of family, and when times get tough they are the ones who pull you through. It often brings out our true feelings, and we say things we might never have said otherwise.

I do feel us growing closer day by day. It is a wonderful feeling for me too. Of course, the best part was the hug. I closed my eyes and you were right there. And you know something? You were right. That is exactly what I needed…you. I guess I've needed that for a long time. So thanks for being there for me. I want you to know that I'm here for you as well, in good times and in bad.

The whole time I was gone, I kept thinking about how much my life has changed. The whole world just looks different to me…it's like seeing everything through new eyes. It has given new meaning to many things. I'm also much happier with "me". And I'm so happy that you're part of my life. I have a lot to be thankful for.

I've been working on the letter to your mom. This is a tough one for me. I don't want to say the wrong thing. I'm trying hard to be sensitive to her feelings. She said some really wonderful things that meant so much to me. I want her to know how much I appreciate that. I want to try to put her mind at ease as well.

Talk to you later, Jeanne

E-MAIL FROM KEVIN TO JEANNE

From: Ksweet1072@aol.com
Date: February 26, 1998 2:04pm
To: Jeanneb1@IBM.net
Subject: Welcome home!

Dear Jeanne,
Welcome home! It seemed like forever since we last heard from you. I am glad things are progressing the way they are. It is so amazing that all of this is happening. I guess in the back of my mind I had always wished for this to happen. You are a wonderful person. I can see so much of you in Karen. Karen is the most precious and beautiful thing in the world to me. I want to thank you for giving this gift to me. She completes me and makes my life so meaningful and joyful.

I really look forward to the day that I get to meet you and Paul. Sometimes I find myself pushing Karen more than I should. I often say "lets call or go and see them." I know it is up to the two of you, but I just can't wait for this reunion to happen. A family can never have enough people, and I am glad that you and Paul will be a part of ours. I am sure Karen will be on shortly to send you her own message. Have a great night and say hello to Paul.
Kevin

From: Jeanneb1@IBM.net
Date: February 27, 1998, 2:04pm EST
To: Ksweet1072@aol.com
Subject: A feel good day

...Kevin is such a sweetheart. His letter was so lovely. I read it to Paul last night when he called. I started a letter to him but I'll have to finish it when I get back from work tomorrow. So in the meanwhile, tell him thanks and give him a big hug for me.

I'll be anxious to get home to check my mail! Bye for now.

Love,
Jeanne

KAREN

The last two months of letters and e-mails had been filled with a lot of excitement and curiosity. Jeanne and I had pretty much learned all we could about each other through this kind of correspondence. It had been good for my soul. Even though I was still very nervous, I knew I could deal with it. Jeanne had been very patient. She never suggested a physical meeting between us, with the exception of sharing her dream of having me in her wedding. I got the feeling she would make Paul wait forever if I didn't suggest it. I knew it was my move. I was ready.

From: Ksweet1072@aol.com
Date: Saturday, February 27, 1998 06:37pm EST
To: Jeanneb1@IBM.net
Subject: A visit

I have been thinking about scheduling a visit for you and Paul. Could you possibly get away and make a trip to Cleveland, perhaps for a weekend? Kevin and I would like to meet you.
Karen

From: Jeanneb1@IBM.net
Date: February 28, 1998 9:37pm EST
To: Ksweet1072@aol.com
Subject: I think it's time

... I just wanted to tell you that there isn't anything that would make me happier than to come to Cleveland! Everything feels right and I think it is time. So we'll talk and figure out when and how it will happen, okay? I'm anxious to share our ideas and thoughts about the whole thing. I've been thinking about it non-stop all day!

Hope to talk soon.

Love,
Jeanne

From: Jeanneb1@IBM.net
Date: February 28, 1998 11:26pm EST
To: Ksweet1072@aol.com
Subject: A bit anxious

Hi, it's me. I'm starting to get a little worried. I thought that I might hear from you by now. I hope that everything is okay. I guess I'm just a bit anxious. We just installed the AOL Instant Messenger, so I think that we'll be able to chat back and forth now. So I'm excited about that. I just hope it works. I thought that it would be a great way for us to talk and make plans about getting together. I'll check my messages when I get up so maybe we can try it out then.

Good night.
XXOO, Jeanne

From: Ksweet1072@aol.com
Date: Saturday, February 28, 1998 11:37pm
To: Jeanneb1@IBM.net
Subject: A visit

Hi. I wasn't sure what your schedule were like or when you would be able to visit. I've been thinking about having you out for my graduation. Actually, if you could come sooner (maybe March or April), we would have a better chance to know each other first. I've already spoken to my parents and they agreed that they had been to two of my graduations already and that you and Paul might want to come in June.
Karen

From: Ksweet@aol.com
Date: Sunday, March 1, 1998 9:47pm
To: Jeanneb1@IBM.net
Subject: A road trip to Cleveland

Hi. We must have been typing our messages to each other about the same time last night.

Kevin's parents are planning to come the last week of March. I finish school March 18th and have nothing planned March 21and 22nd or April 24 to the 26th. Either of those dates works for us.

I know you have to check your schedules, but right now these are the dates that Kevin and I could spend the most time with both of you. Let me know your thoughts.

Karen

From : Jeanneb1@IBM.net
Date: March 1, 1998 11:44 EST
To: Ksweet1072@aol.com
Subject: Making plans

Hi, I was glad to get your message from last night and this morning... The weekend of March 21 was the weekend I had in mind, so I'm glad that looks good for you. Paul said he needs to check his schedule as well.

I was thinking it would probably take us 10 to 12 hours if we drive straight through. Do you think it would be good for us to arrive late on Friday or Saturday morning? I'm thinking that it might be good to stop when we are tired and get a good night's sleep. Then we could get up early in the morning on Saturday and meet up with you then. That way we won't be so exhausted when we arrive. Another option could be to leave on Thursday and spend the night and meet up on Friday evening for dinner. That would give us a little more time together, and we could leave on Monday morning.

Please talk it over with Kevin and see what you think. In the meantime try not to worry about things too much because I know it will all be just fine. I want this to be a happy and joyous occasion that the four of us will share and celebrate together.

Maybe later we could try the AOL Instant messenger. I'll get back online between 4:30 and 5:00. Just keep checking whenever you have time and I will do the same.

Talk to you later, Jeanne

KAREN

It was difficult for me to think of this as a "happy and joyous occasion." It wasn't like a wedding or a baptism. I knew how much it must mean to Jeanne, but my nervousness and sense of caution were making me wonder if I could actually do this. I tried to tell myself that these feelings were natural. I was fearing the unknown. I knew if I cancelled out now, I would break Jeanne's heart, so that was not an option. I gathered my courage and told myself not to be silly. Of course I could do this.

From: Ksweet1072@aol.com
Date: March 3, 1998 6:33pm EST
To: Jeanneb1@IBM.net
Subject: Thinking About The Visit

I have been thinking about your visit. We hadn't discussed where you and Paul would be staying. Normally company stays with us, but to be honest I'm not quite ready for all that in one visit.

I think the day will be overwhelming for us and we'll both need our alone time to digest it all. I hope this okay with you. There are some hotels in the downtown area and in Lakewood that I could gets numbers for you to call.

I hope you understand how I feel.

Talk to you soon.

Karen

I realized that for the first time in our relationship I could say exactly how I felt without the worry of hurting Jeanne's feelings. It was obvious that our relationship had progressed to the level of friendship, even though we had not met yet.

From: Jeanneb1@IBM.net
Date: March 6, 1998 16:39:34 EST To: Ksweet1072@aol.com
Subject: Not to worry

Hi, my response to your letter about "the visit" is ... not to worry! That is absolutely fine with both of us truly! Paul and I had discussed the idea of staying in a hotel. We thought that it might make more sense and would be easier for everyone. So if you hadn't brought it up I would have. Anyway, I am glad you were honest with your feelings.. This is exactly the kind of thing I wanted to talk with you about. I'm definitely into making things as easy and comfortable as possible. I also don't want you to have to worry about food. We can just eat all of our meals out. Now that we've settled that, you can let me know which hotels you would recommend. Are there any nice B&Bs nearby? I like the idea of showing up on Friday and having dinner out together. Just let us know what time to get there.

I'm anxious to see your house, the dogs, and your neighborhood. I would enjoy seeing any photo or wedding albums you might have. I would also enjoy taking a nice walk together so we can be relaxed and have time to talk. What are your thoughts? You mentioned that you wanted to show us around Cleveland, which sounds find to me. Maybe we would have lunch downtown somewhere? Is there anything else special that you had in mind? If so, let's talk later.

My family is very excited about us getting together. I've been e-mailing my two nieces Shannon and Alana, and have been keeping them informed about everything. Alana's comment was, "I think that she is going to be so surprised when she sees how much you both look alike." My sister Kay also thinks that we look a lot alike, but feels that you look a lot like my mom. She was very beautiful when she was young. ...I am closer to my sister Kay because she and I are more alike. We aren't afraid to show our emotions. I see her and Dad twice a week before I go to work. Plus we talk on the phone a lot. She usually calls me or I call her on the day I work, since it is a local call. That gives us time to catch up on all the news. I think I've gotten closer to her since my mom died. I usually talk to my sister Linda at least once a week, but I don't see her quite as often. My nieces are in and out, so I usually see one or two of then when I'm there. They are sweet kids. I love to hug and kiss all of them! As I have gotten older, family has become much more important to me. Are you very close with your sister?

I think that I'll go ahead and send this so you will have some mail when you get home. I'll look forward to chatting with you later.

Love, Jeanne

From: Ksweet@aol.com
Date: Saturday, March 7, 4:57pm
To: Jeanneb1@aol.com
Subject: Being studious

Hi. I was very glad to get your "Not to Worry" e-mail. I feel much more at ease and think it will be more relaxing for us all this way. I have looked up a few hotels in the phone book. It looks like the Day's Inn in Lakewood is the closest to us.

Anyway, I'm getting sick. It is my ears and throat and I'm feeling tired. Kevin, (and my dogs, Hannah and MacKenzie) are all stuck together in a little nap...we truly spoil these dogs.

Well, I'll be working offline for awhile. I'll try to get on later to chat.

Take care, until later -
Karen

From: Ksweet1072@aol.com
Date: Monday, March 9, 1998 5:19pm EST
To: Jeanneb1@IBM.net
Subject: Checking In

...I have two finals next week and then I can relax. My friend Lory is going to have a rubber stamp party and she wants to have it when I can come. She is the friend with whom I do all of my holiday cards. We are very close, even though she is 11 years older than me. She and I have known each other for over eight years. We worked together in Albany. She has really helped me through the last year. I would like for you to meet her one day...

See ya, Karen

KAREN

I thought about my friend Lory. She's my dearest friend. It made me think. Jeanne is not much older than Lory. Age made no difference with my friendship with Lory, so why should it matter with Jeanne?

From: Ksweet1072@aol.com
Date: Friday, March 13, 198 6:22pm
To: Jeanneb1@aol.com
Subject: I'm alive

...I was home sick yesterday, but am feeling better today. I had a chance to read a little more about reunions. The book I'm reading is mostly about the effects that reunions have on birth mothers. How it changes them and makes them feel better. I haven't gotten to any actual reunion stories yet.

All the while, though, I was thinking of you. One birth mother said she never had any other children because she almost felt she would be betraying the child she gave up. She felt that if that child found her and learned that she had raised other children, she wouldn't be able to face the first child. Others immediately married and had other children to make up for the loss of the child they had given up.

Maybe you could share with me why you never married or had other children. That would be something that I would like for us to share. The book has also helped me understand how adopted children think. They mostly asked the same questions as I did: Do I look like someone? What nationallity am I? What religion? I found it very reassuring.

I'll check a little later to see if you are online.

See ya,
Karen

From: Jeanneb1@IBM.net
Date: March 14, 1998 17:34:47 EST
To: Ksweet1072@aol.com
Subject: Snowed In

Hi, I was happy to receive your "I'm alive" message. I missed you! I'm glad that you're feeling better. I think all the stress finally caught up with you and your resistance was low. I know how hard you have been pushing. Anyway, I think that you really needed a good rest. The good news was that your presentation went well...that's great! Now you're on the home stretch!

Did you get snow today? It looked like your area was included on the weather map. It just stopped snowing about ½ hour ago and I'd say we have 9 or10 inches. Paul just went over to the shop to get the plow truck. Now the sun is shining and it looks lovely.

It sounds like the book you are reading would be very good for me too. I'd like to try and find a copy. I've been thinking a lot about your question. Why didn't I ever get married or have other children? I think that it was a combination of a lot of things. I could probably explain it to you better in person, but I'll tell you some thoughts. For a long time, I think I was always afraid that if I had another child, it would bring back all of the painful memories of losing you. I couldn't face that. I didn't know how to react. I also remember having this fear of having another child and then having it taken away from me. None of it makes much sense. I guess I was just confused for a long time and didn't know how to handle it. Deep down I think that what I wanted more than anything else was to find "Mr. Right" and get married and have children. Maybe I was looking for somebody too perfect who doesn't exist. But I don't think that I was ever truly happy with myself because there was always something missing. The emotional scar was very deep, and I never really got over losing you. Anyway, somehow I never felt "right". I didn't want to have another child unless I felt I could provide a happy, secure life. I wanted to be a good mother. I told myself that I couldn't be selfish and just have a child for my own benefit. There were a lot of different factors involved and I think that I'm still trying to figure them out. It would probably be very helpful to me to talk about it with you when we get together. To be continued...

I was wondering if you talked to your mom over the weekend?

I'll be around if you have a chance to say "hi".

Love you, Jeanne

From: Ksweet1072@aol.com
Date: Sunday, March 15, 1998 10:47am
To: Jeanneb1@IBM.net
Subject: A Sunday morning note

Good Morning!

Hi to you and Paul. We received your package yesterday. Thanks for the map of New York City, now I can picture things better when you mention where you are.

Anyway, I did talk to my mom. She received your note, she did share it with me, and it was lovely. I could tell by her voice that she feels better as well.

This is very difficult for my brother. As I mentioned before, he is mentally challenged. I don't think he really understands what being adopted really means. He asked my mom what I was going to do with our family now that my biological mother has found me. My parents are trying to explain things to him. I talked with him on the phone this morning, but not specifically about what is happening. More to just to say hello and let him know I want to talk to him, see what he's up to, and that it will be okay.

I've also been thinking about your letter yesterday regarding never getting married or having children. I could feel the emotions in your words and tried to imagine how you felt, but couldn't. I sat back on the couch and felt sad. I would like to talk with you more about this.

I know it is going to take more than just me. This can be a happy time. We just have to put it all in perspective and go forward.

I was watching the History Channel about the German war and the Jewish death camps. I tell myself that these people had it hard and that they felt real torture and pain. I know it is not exactly the same, but it make me realize how fortunate I am. I am most blessed.

Your letter to mom mentioned that you were actually glad that you were coming in April instead of March. Actually, that weekend is the same date as last year, when I had returned home from vacation and received your form letter. Look how far we have come in a year.

See ya,
Karen

From: Jeanneb1@IBM.net
Date: March 15, 1998 20:47:20
To: Ksweet1072@aol.com
Subject: Reflections

Hi, Thanks for the letter this morning. You always brighten up my day. I just enjoy hearing about the everyday stuff that you are doing. It doesn't have to be anything really special. I never knew how special it could be to have a daughter to share things with.

Every day I keep thinking how wonderful it is to have you in my life. Sharing my feelings with you has helped me more than you will ever know. I have told you things I never told anyone else before. I was just reading an article in *The Harvard Women's Health Watch* to which I subscribe. It was about the importance of resilience in our lives. It discussed the stages of recovery from a significant loss. I have studied psychology in school, so I already knew a lot on this subject. They had different names for the stages: shock and denial, acknowledgment, pain, adjustment, and moving beyond. Anyhow, it made me think. I realize for the very first time in my life that I really feel as though I am able to "move beyond" this experience. I finally have closure. The cloud has finally lifted and now I can see sunshine. According to this article "at this stage, "life has been reconfigured around the loss and can be even better than it was previously." For example, cancer patients often report finding a "higher purpose" in life or a sharper clarity of vision than before their illness. This is exactly how I feel. Finding you has been the most incredible experience for me. In many ways I feel like my life is just beginning. I also feel that my faith has been strengthened. These were just some thoughts from today that I wanted to share with you.

You mentioned that your brother was having trouble understanding things. I was afraid of that. I meant to ask you what he thought about all of this, especially since he is adopted. I figured that it has been an important topic of conversation when they all came to visit on Valentine's Day. I was wondering if he was starting to ask questions about his birth parents. I hope he is okay. I look forward to meeting him and your sister Annie.

There's one other thing that I thought of after I sent you my last letter. I want you to know that what Pat Rutherford told you was true: one of the reasons I didn't want to get married was that I didn't want to change my name so that you couldn't find me. As I mentioned to you before, there were many reasons. However, this was definitely something that I thought about. Especially since I was living in Florida and then California. The other thing that he told you was also true...I wanted for Paul and I to wait to get married because I wanted you to be in my wedding. You had asked me about our wedding plans, and I've been meaning to tell you.

Our dream has been to get married on the property. We were going to get married last year but Paul wanted to wait for the house to be finished and I wanted to wait to find you. I felt that I was getting close. I thought it would be the most wonderful thing in the world to have my daughter be my maid of honor at my wedding! So now the plan is sometime next year. Paul wants a large wedding, but I would rather have something a little smaller. I told him that I think we should spend the money on a nice honeymoon in Europe. So that's the story. I still want to tell you the story of how Paul and I met. It was very romantic, but that will be another letter.

There is something I've been meaning to ask you about. In several of your letters you mentioned how much you think we are alike. Kevin said the same thing. Also you said your mom could see similarities. I was wondering if you could be more specific.

I know you have your test tomorrow and another on Wednesday. So good luck. I'll be thinking of you and anxious to hear how you did.

Lots of Love,
Jeanne

Hi to Kevin!

KAREN

I thought about ways in which Jeanne and I were similar. We have a similar way of expressing our feelings. Our personalities are similar in that we are caring, sensitive people who are always concerned about what others think. We are also very affectionate. I expressed this to Jeanne in my next e-mail which was lost.

From: Jeanneb1@aol.com
Date: Saturday, March 21, 1998 6:42pm EST
To: Ksweet1072@com
Subject: A good day to stay home

Hi, this morning when I woke up, I could hear freezing rain on the windows. I decided that today was a good day to stay home.

I've been going through a lot of old pictures to bring with us when we come. Paul and I also spent several evenings putting the rest of the construction pictures into the album so that we can bring that along as well.

I also came across a book that I bought several years ago, called *The Adoption Reader*. It sounds similar to the book you have. It is a collection of stories written by adopted daughters, birth mothers, and adoptive mothers. I re-read some of them. The stories written by the adopted daughters helped me to understand things better from that perspective. I think they express a lot of universal feelings, like where did I come from? Who do I look like? I'd like to talk to you more about that sometime. I'm curious to know what kinds of things you thought about over the years. I was wondering how old you were when you were told that you were adopted and how it was explained to you. Anyway, I'll bring the book with me when I come.

Paul just got home. He is making a fire. We will probably be online later if you feel like chatting.

Love, Jeanne

From : Jeanneb1@IBM.net
Date: March 22, 1998, 4:52pm EST
To: Ksweet1072@aol.com
Subject: Snowed in again!

Hi, it finally stopped snowing this afternoon. I'd say that we have a good 8 inches or more. It sounds like you are shoveling snow there too, or do you have a snowblower?

Today I've been doing a lot of searches on the Internet about adoptees, birth mothers, etc. There is a ton of information out there. I made copies of a few articles. "The Recovery Process," Post-Reunion", "Preparation Before Contact", "Dealing with Birth mother Grief." I also ordered several books on adoption. I have been reading about the "adoption triad".

I want to learn more and try to understand things from all three perspectives. This has been an incredible process for me. However, I know that you and your mom are also going through your own process of dealing with this. I just want to try to be sensitive to all of that. I think that reading other people's stories will give me some insight into all of that.

Paul just came in and wants me to take a walk with him. Hope you had a nice day! I'll talk to you soon.

Love,
Jeanne

KAREN

I Did answer the last e-mail but unfortunately, it was lost.

From: Jeanneb1@IBM.net
Date: March 23, 1998 20:58:07 EST
To: Ksweet1072@aol.com
Subject: Home alone tonight

...Paul left for the city this afternoon. I guess we missed each other online last night. By the time I checked my mail, it was to late. In your letter it sounded like you were just into relaxing for the rest of the evening.

Today I've been thinking about you a lot. You told me that you had never talked to your parents about your adoption. I was wondering if you ever talked with anyone else about it when you were growing up? The reason I am asking is because now I am beginning to understand just how much of a shock this was to you when you received my form letter. Particularly if you never really discussed it with anyone. I also realize how important it was for you to have this time and to think about this and sort it out.

This morning I continued my search on adoption stuff. After reading stories by others adoptees I have a better understanding of some of the issues, i.e., identity, feelings of loss, not being connected, etc. A lot of stories talked about how as a child adoptees would fantasize about what their birth mother was like. I was wondering if you ever thought about me, and if so, how did you imagine me to be? I found something called "Birthdays, What the Triad Feels". It said, "A birthday for the adoptee is a time to reflect, to take a few minutes of that day to wonder about your birth, about the mother that carried you and through the painful labor gave life to you that day." I guess I really wanted to understand how it felt for you being adopted? I think that it would help both of us if you feel comfortable sharing any of that.

I am also getting very excited about our visit as the day approaches. I think that it is important to continue to read and prepare ourselves as much as possible so we have some idea of what to expect or not to expect. I know that there is going to be some anxiety. But I have a feeling that there will also be a tremendous sense of peace for both of us once we get past that. I know there will be some crying, hopefully lots of hugging, and I hope we can have some fun!

I was wondering what happens next with school? I like to keep up with your schedule. I was also wondering what your work hours are? We have to figure out what time Paul and I should arrive that Friday for dinner. We will probably arrive early and check into the hotel so there won't be any rush. You mentioned that Kevin's parents will be arriving this weekend. It sounds like you have a lot of fun together.

Jeanne

KAREN

I recall trying to picture my birth mother when I was younger. I imagined her as very beautiful, with brown hair and brown eyes, but her face always lacked detail. This was part of the defense mechanism of a young girl. It was like imagining a fairy princess. In the innocence of my childhood, she looked exactly the way I wanted her to look.

From: Ksweet1072@aol.com
Date: Monday, March 30, 1998, 10:17pm EST
To: Jeanneb1@aol.com
Subject: Off to bed

Hi, I had my first class of the new trimester tonight. The teacher didn't keep us the full two hours, thank goodness, because it was awfully warm in the classroom.

We are enjoying Kevin's parents visit. We worked in the yard all day Sunday and then had friends over for a home cooked meal. We grilled out.

We are going to my favorite place, Johnnie's Bar, for dinner Thursday night. I can't wait.

Talk to you soon,
Karen

P.S. I got a B- in my Quant Class (it was hard) and an A+ in my Marketing Management class. So I was pleased all around considering how much time I put into both, plus working.

At this point I wanted to share my grades with Jeanne. I was not sure why, but I wanted her to be proud of me. It seems that another stage of our relationship was evolving. I cared what she thought.

Jeanne and I finally talked on the telephone. Her voice was a bit higher than I expected, but lovely. Ironically, she told me later that my voice was higher than she expected and I sounded much younger to her than she had expected from a 30 year old.

From: Jeanneb1@IBM.net
Date: Thursday, April 16, 1998, 8:21pm EST
To: Ksweet1072@aol.com
Subject: Hi from Paul

Karen,

How are you doing? Jeanne has planned for us to go to Niagara Falls (I think as a cool-down) before arriving to meet you. I feel it might be a good idea for the two of you to talk on the phone again. It may help to remove more of the pressure and expectations.

I have wished to stay on the sidelines being an ear and shoulder for Jeanne. First helping to hold hope and now to support and be there for her. I feel the time you spent writing each other was the best way to get insight into each other's lives. God shows us the vision, and then it's for us to create the path.

I've known from your first letter that things would find themselves in a good place. I hope you are well, and let me know if there is anything we can do to help pave the way.

Paul

From: Ksweet1072@aol.com
Date: Sunday, April 19, 1998 10:59pm EST
To: Jeanneb1@IBM.net
Subject: Sorry we missed you online

We had company until 10:30 this evening. We just tried you after they left and did not get anyone. We had dinner with our friends. My friend's wife and Karen have something in common: they are both adopted. Karen was talking with her for the first time tonight about it. Her father just found out he has cancer, so it was a night for bonding.

Karen is getting nervous about your meeting each other. Just try to be understanding of her emotions. I think this whole process has happened a lot faster than she had anticipated. Have a good night!
Kevin

The Meeting

It was Thursday, April 22, 1997 when we began our road trip to Cleveland. As the day approached I began to feel the anxiety building. I decided it would be a good idea to leave a day early and make an overnight stop at Niagara Falls. This way, I could relax before arriving in Cleveland the next day. I had always dreamed of visiting Niagara Falls, the famous honeymoon destination. I felt the place would have a calming effect on me and help put me in the right frame of mind. I realized this was new territory for all of us, and we would just have to feel our way along. The only thing I could do at this point was trust that my maternal instincts would guide me.

We arrived in Niagara Falls early in the afternoon and checked into a hotel. I had requested a room with a view of the falls. I was very excited, and after we dropped our bags off in the room we got the first glimpse of the falls. We immediately ventured out to get a closer view. It was early spring, and we walked through a beautiful park filled with thousands of tulips in bloom. At the falls, I recognized the spot which I had seen in a picture of a trip my mom and dad had taken to the falls when they were young. I will never forget how I felt when I saw this magnificent site. It was similar to the feeling I got the first time I laid eyes on the Grand Canyon.

Paul and I sat on a bench for a long time, mesmerized by this awesome natural wonder. The sound of the water rushing over the falls was very soothing, just as I had imagined it would be. That night we watched the light show over the falls from our room. We called Karen and Kevin to let them know we had arrived, and told them all about our day.

The next morning we hiked along the trail that leads around the falls. It was a beautiful, warm, sunny spring day. We paused several times along the way to take pictures and capture the magic. Anyone who ever makes a visit to Niagara Falls soon discovers the perpetual rainbow created by the falls' mist.

I couldn't help but think how I was finally reaching the end of the rainbow where dreams are supposed to come true. It was indeed a romantic place. After spending the day there, I felt more relaxed and refreshed. I was experiencing the healing powers of Mother Nature.

That afternoon we checked out of the hotel and headed off to Cleveland. We arrived at the Cleveland hotel before dark. It was a small hotel in a residential neighborhood. We called Karen and Kevin and told them we had arrived. We checked in and took a walk to have a look around. We decided it would be best to try to get to sleep early so we would be rested in the morning. But of course, it was difficult to sleep with so many thoughts racing through my mind. Tomorrow was the big day, the day I had been dreaming of for thirty years. It had been a very long journey and I began to think how much my life had changed. My life was very good now, and I had so much to offer Karen, so many things I wanted to share with her. I prayed that somehow it would all work out for the best and things would go well on our first visit.

I woke up in the morning and went through the motions of getting ready. We made one final call to let Karen and Kevin know we would be there shortly and made sure they were ready. On the way we stopped to pick up a bouquet of flowers and a bottle of wine. We found the right street and began to look for the house in the picture that Karen had sent. We spotted it and parked the car.

Suddenly everything felt larger than life. It was like watching myself in a movie. Am I dreaming? Is this really happening? Every step was a step closer. In just a matter of moments I would touch my daughter for the first time. I felt a bit of fear creeping into my heart and I grabbed Paul's arm. He could sense it too, and he took my hand. I don't think I could have made it any further without him.

I can recall Kevin and I cleaning the house; after all, isn't that what you do when company was coming? But Jeanne and Paul were not just any company. This wasn't a normal Saturday afternoon get- together for tea. I could feel the anticipation building. I had to keep busy as the hour to the reunion got closer. I wanted the house to be perfect. I thought, my home would be part of the first impression of how Kevin and I lived. It was important to me that my home reflected the life we had made together. It was simple and quaint, yet we thought it was very comfortable for a first home.

The next thing was, what do I wear? I didn't want to dress as if this were the social event of the year, but it was monumental. What does one wear on such an occasion? I wanted to be comfortable, so I selected a denim dress with a red cotton blazer and a white floral scarf. I wanted my hair to be perfect. Perfect! Why did it matter so much?. Once more, all I could think of was that I wanted my "natural mother" to be proud of who and what I had become and all that I had accomplished. Even though we had relayed that many times in our letters, I felt it was different now that she was actually going to see my world. I suppose that is why it mattered to me so much.

As the time neared for our meeting, I remember standing at the window watching every car go by on this sunny Saturday in April. As I anxiously waited Jeanne's arrival, I noticed their car driving past our house and parking one block up the street. I could see a tall, slender man get out of the car, walk to the passenger door, and extend his hand. Then Jeanne stepped out of the car, a smile adorning her face. I could see she was wearing a light-colored dress. I thought to myself, she is here; she is finally here and this is really happening. I saw her grab Paul's arm. He pulled her closer to him and took her hand as they started to walk toward the house.

I felt a little fear enter my heart, and I called for Kevin to let him know they had arrived. I gripped Kevin's hand. My heart was beating a mile a minute as she approached. I could see her crossing the street, walking hand-in-hand with Paul. She too looked nervous; I could see her clenching Paul's arm for dear life with one hand while she balanced the bouquet of flowers in the other. Yet her smile had begun to really light up her face as she got closer to my home. She was just as I had imagined, the woman I had conjured up in my head so many years before. Now in real life I could see she was the beautiful woman I had pictured. She was glowing and radiant.

JEANNE

I took one final deep breath. I thought, only a few more steps now, I think I can make it. Kevin greeted us at the front door. We walked in and there she was waiting for me….my beautiful little girl who was all grown up. She had the most beautiful eyes and the sweetest smile I had ever seen. I remember giving her a long hug and of course we both cried. I handed her the flowers. I always tried to imagine how it would actually feel to hold my daughter and to look into her eyes for the first time. I knew it would be very special, but it was difficult to know for sure. Now I knew. It was the most wonderful feeling in the world, and no one could ever take that away from me. When she put her arms around me, her touch reached to the depths of my soul. If I had died right there, I would have died happy. The search was finally over.

KAREN'S REACTION

Kevin went to the door to greet them. I felt as if I couldn't move. Time seemed to stand still for those few seconds as I waited inside. I began to feel overwhelmed and very apprehensive. It was like I was on emotional overload. Then, Jeanne and Paul were walking in the entryway into my living room. Immediately a big smile and two extended arms reached for me and snatched me up. It wasn't really registering for me, but there she was.

I kept looking at her even as I was hugging her. It is really hard to recall the exact words we spoke, but I do remember it was difficult to absorb everything that was happening. Jeanne had no problem pouring out her emotions, which I could clearly feel as we embraced. But I began to feel my cautious side return.

I realize now that during the writing and e-mail process, I had shed some of my cautious tendencies because I was in a comfortable place with our relationship. The actual meeting was different. One has a certain anonymity when communicating in writing. It's like talking to a mental image rather than a real person. But now, it was as if seeing Jeanne for the first time had jolted me back to that same place where I was a year earlier, when this all began. I had the feeling I was starting over.

I realized that our meeting was exactly one year to the day of receiving the form letter, which told me my birth mother was looking for me. And now, here was Jeanne standing in front of me.

We began looking through the photo albums that each of us had brought to share. It was eerie to see the pictures of Jeanne when she was younger; we looked so much alike. The resemblance was remarkable, and for me it helped to take away the surrealist feeling of this relationship and make it real. We spent much of the evening sharing pieces of the past with each other. Paul and Kevin both helped to fill in conversation and make it comfortable for everyone.

The next day, walking through the Metropark with Jeanne, we really began to open up with each other. I felt more comfortable asking about the situation surrounding my birth, Jeanne's relationship with my birth father, her parent's reaction, and how she felt after giving me up. In spite of the fact that she had already shared much of this in the e-mails, seeing her live reaction to my questions was totally different. I wanted to read her face and expressions as she recalled these events, the kind of body language that could never be conveyed in letters and e-mails.

Jeanne answered the questions openly and honestly. I think the saddest thing was to hear that never got to see or hold me when I was born. The drugs from the delivery hadn't worn off, she was still confused, and she said that everything had happened so fast. Papers were flashed in front of her to sign. There was no one to explain what they were, and she was never sure about what was actually happening. I thought to myself how frightening it must have been.

After our walk, we all went to lunch at Westside Brewing Company and then decided to take Jeanne and Paul on a tour of Cleveland. We showed them the downtown where Kevin and I worked, as well as other notable sites. Later we had dinner at one of our favorite neighborhood spots. After dinner we went back to the house to say our goodbyes.

We agreed to continue to e-mail each other, and decided to also continue to exchange phone calls. However, we did not plan another meeting or trip to see each other. I think that the weekend had been overwhelming enough for both of us, and that we needed a little time to reflect on it.

As we said our goodbyes, I was feeling good about how things had gone. I also felt relieved, like the relief you feel after winning a big game or making an important presentation at work. It all seemed like everything was going to work out and that we could now move forward.

THE OBITUARY

Webster's dictionary defines a coincidence as an accidental or remarkable occurrence of events, ideas etc. at the same time, suggesting but lacking a casual relationship. Several such coincidences occurred in the course of the search and reunion between Jeanne and myself.

Alma Biedrzycki

HUDSON — Funeral services for Alma B. Biedrzycki of Elizaville, who died Sunday, will be tonight at 8 at Bates & Anderson Funeral Home.

Interment will be at the convenience of the family.

Memorials may be made to the Southern Columbia Ambulance Squad, Livingston 12541.

It was Christmas of 2002 when my mother was putting up her Christmas tree. In 1994, eight years earlier, she had wrapped some of the Christmas tree ornaments in newspaper, and now decided she would use those particular ornaments for this year's tree. When she opened the box, she sat for a moment to read this old newspaper, curious about some of the things that had happened in her community eight years ago. The newspaper opened directly to the obituary section, and the name "Alma Biedrzycki" leapt out at her. It was the obituary for Jeanne's mother.

Mom couldn't wait to call me and tell me about this amazing coincidence. She sent me the clipping and I was in awe when I read it. The newspaper had been stored in her attic long before Jeanne had ever contacted me. I could not help but feel that my birth grandmother, who had died on Christmas Day so long ago, had chosen this way to contact me. I felt the "circle" was now complete.

There are many other coincidences which occurred during this journey. Although none are quite as direct as the obituary, I think they are worth mentioning.

Jeanne and I both grew up on dairy farms

Jeanne and my mother, are both registered nurses.

Jeanne and I were the "middle" child of three children

Jeanne's heritage is half Polish. My mother is Polish and was exposed to Polish foods and cooking by her mother

1994 was a significant year in both our lives. Jeanne's mother died suddenly, bringing her closer to her remaining family and I get married and move to Cleveland, away from my family.

Jeanne's father cutout an article about the local adoption reunion of a 37 year-old woman and gave it to Jeanne.

My mother cutout the exact same article and mailed it to me. Both parents did this within in days of each other, of course unknown to the other.

Our reunion was exactly one year from the date I received Jeanne's form letter in the mail. This was not planned!

As I write this story now, it has been a great experience to re-read all of our e-mails and talk again with Jeanne just as openly and honestly as we did five years ago. It was like living the experience all over again, but this time without all of the cautiousness and worry about how it would all turn out. It also made me reflect on what we had experienced together, little things I had forgotten or missed as I was living through it all, or on something that had been overlooked. Re-reading the hospital records and re-thinking again the circumstances of my birth, recalling just how busy everything in my life was at the time, yet things really did work out well in the end.

I remember re-reading one of Jeanne's e-mails in particular, entitled "A New Day," which she wrote in February of 1998. It read, " I just wanted everything to be nice for all of us and it is my hope that one day we could all feel like a family." I can honestly say I think that we have accomplished this. My family, and Jeanne and Paul, all get along just as if Jeanne had been in my life long ago. No more does anyone feel threatened or wonder what is going to happen next. And now, as we move ahead, these feelings have all but disappeared for us.

At some point in time we became a family. My husband, Kevin feels, I have two families who love me: my lifelong family, and my natural one. Kevin's parents are divorced and his two sets of parents get along equally as well as mine. None of us has to worry about getting together for the holidays or my son Brendan's birthday; everyone gets along wonderfully. We have started an annual post Christmas dinner at my home with my mom and dad, and Jeanne, and Paul. This past year, I heard my dad tell Jeanne, "Having you come into our lives has been a positive experience." I agree. I could not have wished for any better outcome.

After our first meeting, I felt that I could move forward with my life and that things were good, so Jeanne and I planned a special trip to New York City. This was my graduation present from her, and also a big step we were taking together. I was quite excited to see the other part of Jeanne's city life. I had never really been to New York City before and was looking forward to exploring it with her.

This trip became the first of many trips we took together. They became "excursions" that just the two of us shared. We enjoyed the theater, the museums, Central Park, and just endlessly walking Manhattan's streets to see where they would take us. I felt Jeanne and I grew closer on these trips. It was just the two of us in the sea of people flooding the busy streets, subways, and attractions. It is hard to describe, but this was our private time away from our normal day-to-day life that gave us a chance to explore a city, and each other, at the same time.

Since we moved back to the Northeast, we were able to spend more time together. It feels very comfortable and natural. We enjoy many of the same hobbies and we continually think up ways that allow us to spend more time doing things we enjoy, such as crafts, business ideas, etc. I guess we feel life has given us a second chance, and the people in it are the most important gift. We don't want to squander time and get caught up in the rat race of always trying to get the next big promotion or going on luxury vacations. Our conversations always seem to come back to the simple pleasures: less stress, spending quality time raising my son Brendan, and the basic fundamentals of life, which to me is my family.

Jeanne is part of my life now. I feel blessed that I have both my mom, and Jeanne in my life. I am proud to be their daughter.

I find it hard to believe that it has been five years since my reunion with Karen. So much has happened during this time. I can still remember the intense feelings and confusion as we all tried to adjust to this new situation. These were completely uncharted waters for everyone in the triad as well as for the rest of the immediate family.

In the beginning, it was difficult to know what to say or do next. Karen and I walked so carefully for a long time, and felt as if we were on an emotional roller coaster. Neither of us was quite sure where we would end up. I could only hope that with time, patience, and love one day it would all feel comfortable for everyone. The time we spent writing this book has given me an opportunity to reflect upon the past and remember how we were desperately struggling to reconnect and find all the missing pieces. Getting to know each other was a slow process. Even though we are intimately connected, the feeling of being "family" did not happen automatically. We had to move carefully from one stage to the next. We had to learn to crawl before we could walk. We had to rethink "family roles" and "who is family?"

I slowly began to realize that family can include anyone who loves us unconditionally and is always there for us in good times and bad. It is family that shares special traditions. We feel like "family" by spending time together and sharing all those special moments in our lives. When I think back on the happiest memories of my mother, I think of the times when we did simple things together, like baking cookies. This is what I wanted with Karen. I decided it wasn't too late for us. We have the whole future ahead of us, where anything is possible.

During the past five years I have tried to focus on creating many happy memories with Karen. I wasn't there when she was growing up, but I'm here now and I want to make the most of it. I have decided that my time is the most important gift I can give her. Looking back, I would say that in the past five years we have done more exciting things together than some people do in a lifetime. My “Karen memory” book is slowly filling up, and there are many more pages to go. We have achieved a new level of comfort that goes beyond what I ever imagined. In many ways, she has become my best friend, but at the same time she definitely feels like a daughter. I know that I share her with her parents, Mary Lou and Harold, but I feel we have also found our own places and feel comfortable and secure knowing that certain things will never change.

My feelings of loss are definitely subsiding and are being replaced with a new sense of contentment, knowing that Karen and I have a future together. I am happy and secure now that I know we are back in each other’s lives for good. It amazes me to think that we can sit down together and talk openly about this whole experience. It is very liberating to feel as though we have transcended all of the emotional confusion of the past and moved beyond it.

Our relationship continues to evolve. We now look for ways to spend more time together and make the most of every minute. We never take anything for granted, and count our blessings every day. We still e-mail each other all the time and talk on the phone several times a week. Now that Karen and Kevin have moved back east, we were able to spend some of the Christmas holidays having fun together making gifts for family and friends. For the past several months I have been going to her house every week to work on writing this book. I would periodically take breaks to play trains and read to my grandson, Brendan, who is another gift from God. I have promised to take him for a ride on a real train to New York City when he is older. Now he reaches out and takes my hand and looks forward to my next visit.

Karen called this morning to read the beautiful piece she had written to be included in the final chapter of this book. She also wanted to tell me about an idea she has for writing a children's book for older adopted children. I was very touched by what she had written and her ability to be so completely open and honest with her feelings. I smiled and thought to myself that everything has really come full circle. Look at how far we have come.

As I sit at my computer and write the final chapter of our book, I look out at my beautiful view of the reservoir and snow-covered mountains. I can see clearly now and the future looks bright. Now I really do have everything. I have found the missing pieces, the picture is complete. Now we are a family.

EPILOGUE "AND A CHILD SHALL LEAD THEM"

At my Grandson Brendan's third birthday party, I looked around at the people. Here were Karen and Jeanne; Jeanne's fiancé Paul; Mary Lou and Harold, Karen's adoptive parents; Karen's husband my stepson, Kevin; Kevin's mother Linda (my wife); Kevin's father Larry and his wife Sue; Kevin's half-sister, Melissa; Karen's brother David (who is also adopted); Karen's sister, Annie (biological to Harold and Mary Lou); and a variety of other friends and family.

What a group, I thought to myself. Polish, German, Italian, Irish, Anglo-Saxon; Roman Catholic, Protestant, and Jewish; related, inter-related, not related at all. And then I looked at Brendan and thought of the Biblical phrase, "A child shall lead them." In his innocence, unfettered by the learned behavior of adults, he saw only grandmas and grandpas. Unaware that I am his step-grandfather, that Sue is his step-grandmother, that Mary Lou and Harold are his adoptive grandparents and that only three grandparents are biologically connected to him; he doesn't care. He only knows that we all love him. And that he loves all of us. The person with the smallest heart has room in it for us all. He proves to us that we *can* love one another, and it's in this spirit that we can overcome anything.

Then I thought about Jeanne's dream which was about to come true. She and Paul have set the date and will be married at their home shortly. Karen will be the matron-of-honor. And a little bonus from God: Brendan will be the ring-bearer at Grandma Jeanne's wedding.

The Grandparents

Top row: Harold Leiser, Lawrence Sweet
Middle Row: Mary Lou Leiser, Paul Cohen, Sue Sweet
Bottom Row: Lewis & Linda Elia, Jeanne Biedrzycki,
Brendan, Karen & Kevin Sweet

The Wedding

Honoring Our Love
In Marriage

Jeanne and Paul

August 10, 2003

OSIO
Shokan, New York

Ashokan Spring

**The Dream Comes True – Jeanne and Paul are Married
Karen Sweet is the Matron of Honor**

The Wedding Party
Paul Keller, Best Man – Karen Sweet, Matron of Honor
Taylor DiCapua and Carly DiCapua, Flower Girls
Brendan Sweet, Ring Bearer

As Usual, Brendan Sweet Steals the Show

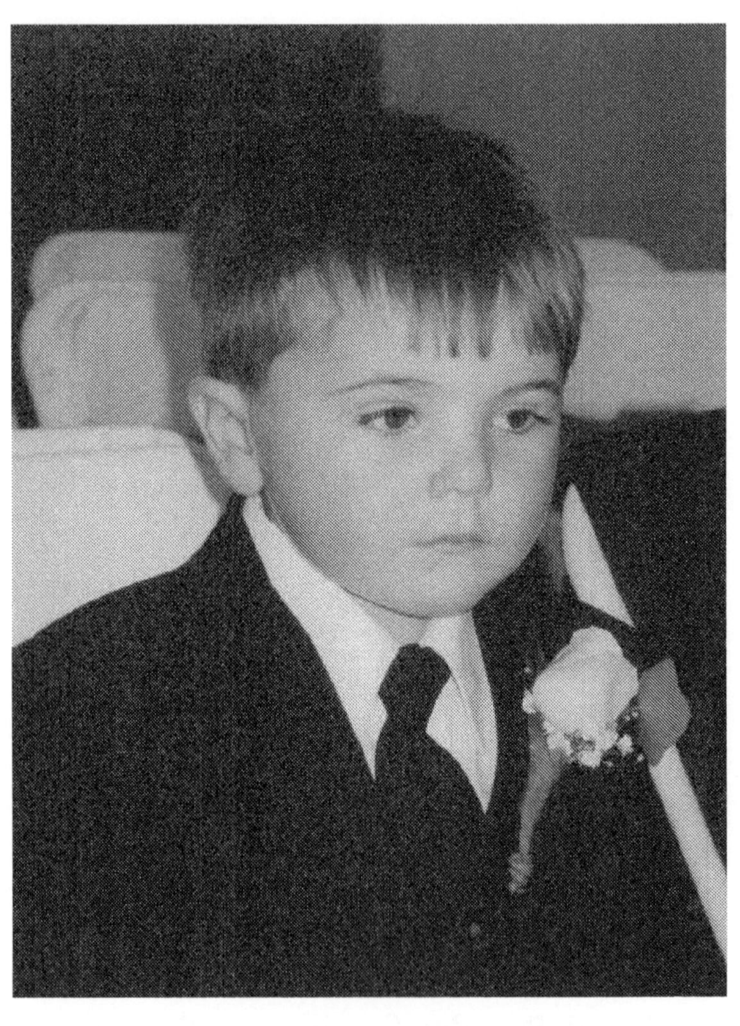

Brendan Sweet, August 10th, 2003
Age 3

www.ingramcontent.com/pod-product-compliance
Ingram Content Group UK Ltd.
Pitfield, Milton Keynes, MK11 3LW, UK
UKHW041847190726
13854UKWH00002B/759

9 781412 007955